THE FORTEA

Bizarre Behaviour

THE FORTEAN TIMES BOOK OF

Bizarre Behaviour

COMPILED BY IAN SIMMONS

ILLUSTRATED BY ED TRAQUINO

JOHN BROWN PUBLISHING

First published in Great Britain in October 1998
by John Brown Publishing Ltd, The New Boathouse,
Bramley Road, London W10 6SR, UK.
Tel 0171 565 3000. Fax 0171 565 3050.

ISBN 1-902212-037

Printed and bound in the UK.

CONTENTS

"There's nowt queer as folk", they say and looking at the clipping files at the Fortean Times, I can only agree. Our "Human Behaviour" file is about the biggest of the lot and bears witness to almost the entire spectrum of human ingenuity, duplicity, tragedy, stupidity and insanity.

The news is basically about what people do, and in many cases what people do is very, very odd indeed. Amid the headline stories about politicians, celebrities, criminals and royalty, there is an undercurrent recording the doings of more humble individuals, their tragedies and triumphs, losses and achievements, but also their madness, eccentricity and surreal logic, and these are what I have gathered here. A number of regular publications run "weird story" columns, proportedly culled from the press, just as these are, but which are, in fact, heavily fictionalised, with participants assigned silly names and with "humourous" quotes attributed to them. In truth, however, you can't better reality - no matter what some columnist might make up, there is always a real story out there which tops it effortlessly, I mean, who could fake the guy who peered into old people's homes dressed as the Grim Reaper, the person who awoke one morning to find her car completely wallpapered, or the woman who would steal babies from their mothers and breast feed them in the street. Extraordinary stuff, and it happens around us every day!

Many of these tales are classics which have appeared in the Fortean Times over the years, but a whole load more are drawn from our vast archives, which we've not had the space to fit in previously. Whether they are all true is hard to say, what is certain is that all these stories have appeared in the press as true at some time. We don't have the resources to check on every one, but we do provide the source references for each story which can be found at the back of the book so you can judge for yourself. Even so, the press is not above recycling old human interest stories, perhaps with the names and locations altered, or printing known "Urban Legends" as fact. Where I suspect this to be the case here, I've flagged the story as a probable UL.

I must, of course, pay tribute to the legion of people worldwide who have actually taken the trouble to clip stories like these from their local papers and sent them in to the Fortean Times, or have posted them of the Internet's Fortean Mailing List. Without them, there'd be no books like this. Please keep them coming!!!! All human life is here - read and enjoy!

IAN SIMMONS

CHAPTER ONE

Over The Edge

Insanity can usually explain the weirdest excesses of human behaviour - but some occurrences seem to be thoroughly rational, yet utterly inexplicable.

TRAFFIC JAMS formed on the A2 in Kent as forensic experts searched for clues after someone blew up two deserted telephone boxes near Canterbury. Powerful enough to kill anyone standing nearby, the bomb was planted by someone who neither gave a warning nor claimed responsibility afterwards, leaving police baffled as to the reason for the blast. Possibly linked is the powerful home-made bomb which was used to blow up a bubblegum machine in Falmouth a few years before, again with no warning or claim of responsibility.

A MAN returning to his mini parked in Shaftsbury Place, Brighton was surprised to find someone had broken into it...and attached an anti-theft lock to the steering wheel. He had to call firemen to release the vehicle.

THIS INCONVENIENCE almost pales into insignificance compared to that suffered by Albert Quirino of Nice, France. Over a three year period someone locked him and his wife out of their house, cellar and garage on over 60 occasions by repeatedly putting padlocks on them. The mysterious lock fiend left no clue as to the reasons for his activities, nor could Albert think of anyone who might hold a grudge against him leading them to do this, but ended up carrying bolt-cutters everywhere with him to deal with the problem. He even installed a video system to try and nail the phantom padlocker and end the frustration. "It's the absolute limit having to break into your own home," Albert complained.

AMANDA MURGETT was forced to change all the locks on her house in Winter Close, Yarm, after inexplicable goings on while she was on holiday. Returning after a month away, she was surprised when one neighbour asked her about the cars parked in her drive and another enquired if she'd been letting the house out. It seemed that first four people, then a couple in their 20's had been living in the house while she was away, arriving after working hours and leaving in the morning. She checked her phone bill for clues, but found no calls had been made, nothing had been damaged or stolen and there were no signs of a break in. The Black Horse Estate Agent who were selling the house for Miss Murgett confirmed that the keys they held for her had remained in their safe throughout her absence, and police said they could do nothing as no theft or damage had occurred.

IN CEDAR RAPIDS, Iowa, fifteen trees in a city park were mysteriously fitted with doorknobs and locks overnight. According to police a white ribbon was tied to each tree about seven feet off the ground, and on each tree about three feet up doorknobs were installed on opposite sides, as if to suggest someone could open a door on one side of the tree, pass through and exit on the other side.

FIVE TIMES in four years a bridal gown and bridesmaid's dresses were left hanging from trees in a Birkenhead park, on one occasion twice within a fortnight. Always left overnight, the immaculate outfits were found by passers by in the morning. "I think it is the same person doing this because the dresses are always left in the similar places - and hanging in a similar fashion" said park ranger Dave Cavanagh, "we would love to know why this person is doing it."

AUTHORITIES in Raleigh, North Carolina were having trouble identifying a man discovered in a hospital car park wearing only a nappy and a t-shirt. He was discovered sitting on a blanket, sucking his thumb and playing with toys. Attached to him was a note saying his name was Matthew and he was 26. Some headway was made when South Carolina police recalled a similar case in 1989 when a man in his early 20's wearing a nappy and a flannel shirt was found outside an addiction treatment centre clutching a teddy, although it was unclear whether the two cases involved the same person.

AT GRAVESEND in Kent, an unidentified man drove up to a McDonald's restaurant - and dumped a live sheep, while in Japan, it was bodiless pigs which kept popping up. 150 severed pig heads were abandoned over a two-year period in Omiya, a Tokyo suburb, baffling police. Annual pig heads sightings grew exponentially between 1992, when there were just five reports, through to 1994 when there were 16. Police remained confused as to the motive as pigs heads are delicacies in Japan and are usually cooked, not thrown out.

FURTHER CONFUSION occurred in Norfolk, where bank bosses put up a £10,000 reward after someone broke into four Barclay's branches throughout the county, but made no attempt to steal any cash. Likewise, confusion reigned in Auckland, New Zealand after someone removed nearly two metres of soil from a 60-year-old grave in the city's Hillsborough Cemetery. The soil was carefully dug out of the grave of Patrick Mathew Mullins, 42, who died in 1932, but no attempt was made to interfere with his remains.

IN CHIPPENHAM, Wiltshire, police were called when a man caused chaos on the busy A350 dual carriageway by practising his cricket stroke with a bat in the middle of the road. He had vanished by the time they arrived.

A BURGLAR broke into a woman's home in Australia and deliberately glued the side of his face to her foot. Cops were stuck for a motive. In Polegate, Sussex, cops were also confused when a house owner claimed someone had broken in and watched a video. Nothing was taken and there was no sign of forced entry, but a video which did not belong to anyone in the house had been left in the machine.

YET MORE baffled cops were to be found in Christchurch, New Zealand, when faced with an apparent trend among early risers in the city - walking home appliances instead of dogs. On 7 May 1996 a man walking his dog in the Parklands saw two fellow early risers trying to "walk" an oven. Two days later, a woman answered a loud knock at her door at 5.15am to be confronted by a man holding a colour TV set. He said he was having difficulty finding his way out of her property and appealed for help. She obliged and then checked that the TV set was not hers. Ten minutes later, police, called to an unrelated matter on a neighbouring property, found the man, still clutching his television. Inquiries revealed the TV belonged to the man, but he could not explain why he was wandering around in the dark with it. "It has left us wondering if there are not enough dogs to go around" said Senior Sergeant Kortegast.

IN RIO DE JANEIRO it was the turn of the residents of the Parada de Lucas slum to baffle law enforcement. On 26 September 1995 they all came out at once and painted all the buildings pale green. Police suspected that the order came from local drug barons hoping to confuse them - obviously with some success.

POLICE in Hamilton, Ontario found more than 1,000 shoes in a trash bin - all brand new, all Reeboks. And all, except one, for the left foot. Constable Mark Taylor said the shoes, sizes 9 through to 11, included runners, hiking boots, and sandals worth about $120,000 retail. Officers suspect that the shoes were stolen and later discarded, but they haven't a clue why a thief wouldn't keep pairs. Perhaps some mischief was afoot. "We've heard all the jokes," said Taylor with a sigh.

A MYSTERY which has vexed many people is the single shoe by the side of the road. Where do they come from ? "I have tried imagining cyclists losing a shoe somehow and carrying on along the road regardless, wearing only one," wrote KGF Perry in the Sussex Evening Argus "Is there a nationwide Shoe Dropping Club, perhaps ?" If he had looked at which foot they came from, he might have solved Constable Taylor's problem.

DEFINITELY paying attention to which foot shoes were from were ornithologists in the Netherlands and Scotland, who have shown that Dutch people more often lose their left shoes at sea, while Scots more often lose their right ones. The comparison began when Dr Mardik Leopold made a remark at an international seabird conference in Glasgow that due to some unknown physical process, left, rather than right shoes were predominantly washed ashore in the Netherlands. Martin Heubeck followed this up. While counting dead birds along 300 miles of Scottish coastline he began counting shoes as well. While the Dutch found 63.5 per cent of intact footwear came from the left foot, Heuback turned up 59.6 per cent of right ones on Shetland's shores. In addition, he found that where only the soles remain, there were more left footers on the east coast of Shetland, than the west. He planned to look into this further.

EQUALLY INEXPLICABLE is why, for many years, all over the USA, old tennis shoes have been tied together and flung over telephone wires, where they sometimes dangle for years. This piqued the curiosity of Moira Smith, a folklorist at the University of Miami. She asked some students about it, and someone suggested that the sneakers went up when someone lost their virginity or made a sexual conquest, but she also thought this could be a made-up tradition to explain the shoes. She reckoned "People do it because they see other people do it. And then people like us start thinking there has to be a reason for it." None of Ms Smith's respondents had seen anyone throwing sneakers over a wire though. "So maybe it's aliens" she ventured.

PASSERS-BY were astonished by the sight of a man, one arm handcuffed to a tree and blood on his face, shouting, kicking and apparently trying to climb up a branch of the tree at North Beach, Durban, South Africa. A beach inspector said the blood on his face was from a self-inflicted cut made by throwing a stone up in the air and letting it fall on his forehead. He was unable to offer an explanation for his actions.

ALSO INDULGING in inexplicable activity was Billy Dodson, of Jacksonville, Florida. He had gone into a church while scantily dressed, placed pamphlets on the pulpit and walked out: later he was seen ramming his car into the church doors, apparently annoyed at the building being closed. He was arrested after sitting in his car and staring at the church for hours. After incriminating himself in a conversation with a cell-mate, he was also accused of a series of acts at city hall where chairs had been overturned in a conference hall and a chess king placed on the head table, on top of a religious pamphlet on which he had written "He is risen" and "OB1-K". The baffling notation "OB1-K" was also found on scraps of paper left in the mayor's desk on the 14th floor. Dodson told investigators that "OB1-K" stood for "Oh boy, one king" but declined to explain further.

EVERY SUNDAY throughout September and October 1997, a woman ran across the lawn of Richard Clothier in Pocatello, Idaho, pausing only to taunt him and empty her bowels. Finally, losing patience, he photographed her in the act and was surprised when the woman - whom he claims never to have met - was identified as a local primary school headmistress, Lyla Ann Wolfenbarger, 46. Needless to say, she denies the charges.

A MAN of 63 was arrested after allegedly breaking into the home of an 83-year-old woman in the Brisbane suburb of Yeronga. She woke at about 5am to find someone licking her face. The man fled when she screamed.

A MYSTERY MAN who claimed to be working for the council took a chainsaw to an entire wood of 200 mature sycamores and alders along the A167 Great North Road outside Durham - and just left them lying there. Police were stumped for a motive. "Before he arrived there was an avenue of 15-year-old trees which had grown to a height of about 20ft (6m) with the trunks about 10in (25cm) thick," said council spokesman Andrew Jackson. "Now there is nothing left."

CHAPTER TWO

Family Fortunes

If people are going to behave strangely, it usually begins in the family

STURE LINDSTROM a fisherman from Gothenburg, Sweden, was taken to court after spanking his wife with a live eel. He was fined £30 - for cruelty to the eel. However, the abandoned wife of a New York man got her own back on her two-timing husband by writing "very small penis" in the distinguishing marks section of his passport. Immigration officials helpfully pointed this out to him as he returned from Paris with his mistress.

IVAN and Doris Weeds celebrated 43 years of marriage without talking to each other. The couple ceased talking shortly after marrying in Melbourne, Australia, but have stayed together and claim that they are still in love. Prolonged silence is more usually grounds for divorce. In Bielefeld, Germany Ernst Horst spoke an average of 3.5 words a day to his wife over a two-month period. His wife Suzanne said "We never have any rows because he never says anything." She kept a notebook, in which his longest recorded utterance was: "This coffee tastes like dishwater," and when asked for a divorce he simply scribbled "I agree."

IN FRANCE, Andrea Puymartin divorced her husband Yves because he kept on snapping her bra strap in church. "He thought it was really funny - but I didn't" she explained. Kitty Charteris, of Salt Lake City, USA, decided she'd had enough of her husband when he refused to stop snipping off bits of her hair as she slept. He stuck it on puppets he made and sold in his toy shop. In Stuttgart, Germany, Wilhelm Schultz also had trouble with his wife in bed. He threw in the towel when his 37-year-old wife Anna insisted her male psychiatrist should share their bed with them - she claimed it was so he could interpret anything Wilhelm said in his dreams. Elsewhere in Germany, Helga Briemer of Giessen got shot of her husband Rolf after six months of sleeplessness brought about by his insistence on eating crunchy celery in bed throughout the night. And finally, in Houston, Texas, an unhappy husband was granted a divorce because his wife insisted that every time he arrived home he should kiss her - then her mother, then each of their three cats.

ISRAEL'S most stubborn man, a Yemeni named Yahiya Avraham died in December 1994, after spending more than 40 years refusing to say the three simple words needed to divorce his wife - "I am willing". Israeli law requires both parties to agree to a divorce, and Yahiyua's wife Ora demanded one in 1950 on the grounds that he treated her like a chattel. He was thrown in jail in 1962 for refusing to say the words, but this did not break his resolve and he vowed never to co-operate; he remained there for the rest of his life. Delegations visited him regularly to try and persuade him to relent - in 1993 he withstood the entreaties of seven rabbis for two hours. They offered him freedom, a fancy apartment and religious blessings, one sang melancholy Yemeni songs to try and soften the man's heart. All he would say was "Can't do it, can't do it, go away." "He's destroyed my life, may his name be destroyed" his wife said in 1993. "I haven't seen his ugly puss since 1967 and I hope I never see him again."

ALAIN AND CLAUDINE Dubert were rushed to hospital with stomach pains after secretly adding arsenic to each other's drinks for months at their home in Cherbourg, France. Police discovered that each had taken out huge insurance policies on the other. In a remote canyon in Nebraska a 23-year-old woman slashed her boyfriend's throat. The man then wrestled the knife away from her and slashed her throat in return. The couple then crawled back to their van, smoked some dope and waited to die. A passing logger found them stoned and bleeding and hauled them down to hospital in Brewster. The aptly named Okanogan County Sheriff, Jim Weed, intended to issue assault charges "because this is not their first domestic dispute."

MARITAL DISINTEGRATION is rarely clean and simple, all sorts of unpleasantness happens when people break up - in Florida a man needed mouth-to-mouth resuscitation after his 21 stone wife sat on his face during a row, while a New Zealand man succeeded in killing his estranged wife by stabbing her in the stomach with a frozen sausage when they argued. A Californian man, on the other hand, was arrested for spousal abuse after savagely beating his partner with a frozen squirrel.

CHAPTER TWO

In Virginia a women found her missing pet outside her door - it had been killed and stuffed by her estranged husband.

A FEMALE bus passenger in Dover was overheard telling her friend how she had just taken her spaniel to the vet, who had diagnosed it as having diabetes. "I can't understand it," she said "There have never been any diabetics in my family or my husband's."

A YOUNG Egyptian man fainted in horror on his wedding night when he lifted the veil of the woman he'd married to find it concealed an unknown woman of 45 instead of his 18-year-old fiancee. The unattractive older woman "looked nothing like his intended partner" reported the Al Akhbar newspaper. As soon as he regained his senses the bridegroom went to the police to file a complaint against his in-laws for cheating him.

FRANCINE WICKERMAN of North Dakota spent 30 years in a bomb shelter - kept there by her jealous husband who locked her in and convinced her that the world had been destroyed by nuclear war. Her ordeal only came to light when she was found following her husband Joseph's death.

ANGRY COWBOY Ross Howard of Denver, protesting about men being allowed to marry men, was refused a licence to marry his horse. The hitch was a technicality; the law says three-year-olds need parental consent. Better luck was had by pregnant Evangeline Guico, 21, in Manila. She was allowed to marry her boyfriend Marlon Manalac - even though the groom was dead. A few days before the ceremony he had been found shot dead by an unknown assassin in a suburb of the Filipino capital. The groom's father, police major Alfonso Manalac, arranged for a minister of the Aglipayan Church, a Filipino

Catholic schismatic denomination, to preside over the ceremony at which Guico said her nuptial vows and sprinkled holy water over the groom's corpse as he lay in his coffin.

IN CHINA dead people getting married can cause considerable problems. In 1991 villagers were reported to be exhuming female relatives and taking them home to prevent the remains being stolen and sold as 'ghost brides', following the arrest of two men for digging up the bodies of six women and selling them to families of men who died unmarried. In another case a dead woman undertook an eight-day journey across China to be married to a man who died a bachelor. The man's family employed professional 'matchmaker for the dead' Zhang Jiahua, 44, to find a suitable match for their relative. He dug up a corpse, which had been dead two years, in Sichuan and was taking it to be buried with the man in Shanxi when railway officials searched his baggage and found the remains. Ghost marriages have a long tradition in China, but it is usually only the spirits who marry, in effigy form - these characters seem to have been taking things rather literally.

MARY MARLEY'S grisly secret was only discovered after she died. Police were called to the 70-year-old's maisonette when she failed to answer the door to neighbours. Mrs Marley was found dead in the lounge, but the real surprise came when they went up stairs - in her bedroom they found the skeleton of her 50-year-old lover tucked up in bed. He had died there 12 months earlier and she had kept him ever since. Rather less conscientious was oilman Geoffrey Walter, who was being sought by Thai police after he left his late wife's skull on a bus. They wanted him to collect it as it was upsetting the bus company.

EGYPTIAN police arrested a 48-year-old widow carrying her husband's skull out of a cemetery in Menofiya province because she missed his company. She told police that her husband, who died in 1992, asked her in a dream to take him back to their home. She sifted through his grave, but was only able to find the skull. Acting on a similar impulse Muhammed Tofizuddin, 55, dug up his wife's skeleton in Bangladesh, washed the bones and tenderly arranged them on a table. Since his wife, Gulbahar Banjla, died two years earlier, he had seen her every night in his dreams.

ALSO INCITED by dreams a Ugandan woman exhumed her husband's corpse on a daily basis and took it home "to enjoy the sunshine". Reports stated that the woman's husband, when he'd been buried for a year, began appearing in her dreams lamenting that it was chilly in the grave and requesting to be dug up for a "warming stint". According to the Uganda Star newspaper "Each day, when the sun rises, the widow gets the corpse out to bask and returns it after a considerable period". The woman, from Muwuggwe village, 75 miles west of Kampala, was helped in the task by her children.

THE JAPANESE EFFICIENCY CORPORATION rents families by the hour or day to those who live alone, offering shopping companions to housewives, sympathetic ears to stressed-out executives, even people to scold for those who are dying to tell someone off, but can't, inhibited by Japan's culture of restraint. Employees are ranked from seventh to first class depending on acting ability. Customers have to be wealthy as the service costs up to £300 an hour. There can be problems, though: the police were called when Mr and Mrs Tancha from Okinawa, both over 80, began to abuse and beat three rented 'grandchildren' for their disrespectful behaviour.

CHAPTER THREE

Proud To Be Different

England is famed for it's eccentrics, but by no means has a monopoly on them

DURING HIS divorce hearing a man in Cologne was found to have a 3ft long Japanese sword concealed in his trousers. The man, who also carried a loaf, tomatoes and butter, claimed he was going to use the sword to make sandwiches while he waited for his case to come up.

A MOST Boring Hobby contest in the USA was won by Mildred Sherrer, 69, who comprehensively beat all other entrants due to her obsession with collecting the caps from vinegar bottles - all of the same brand. The retired teacher has more than 2,000 of the things and began her collection

10 years ago when she started pouring vinegar into her bath to soothe her arthritis. Her ultimate goal is to paint them white and make sets of draughts out of them. In India flute player Ramen Naskar devoted his spare time to trying to hypnotise rats. After 12 years of this he claims he can now make them dance.

MEANWHILE in Australia, Adam Newman has three arks sitting in readiness in Sydney harbour after having received a mysterious message telling him the world was going to end in a great flood. He has also waterproofed his home to give it greater buoyancy for the forthcoming deluge. Also preparing for the Apocalypse was John Roeleveld, 72, from Eerbeeck, Holland, who claimed that God had told him to collect and mount two of every species in preparation for the imminent end of the world. More than 40 years ago God promised that his collection would rise up and live again after Judgement Day, and that the scrap iron fragments and old furniture that littered his garden would also be made new. When police finally raided Roeleveld's house in response to complaints from neighbours they found an amazing warren of concrete bomb shelters in the backyard of his shabby home packed with more than 250,000 stuffed animals and birds. These included crocodiles, ostriches, kangaroos, panthers, apes, a bear, an elephant skull and a camel. Some had been stuffed in the last century, but most were the work of Roeleveld himself. Many belonged to protected species and it was not clear how they had come into his possession. There were also thousands of eggshells, bones and insects preserved in formaldehyde. Roeleveld wasn't upset when 40 police and firemen began removing his collection. "They will return to me of their own accord," he said. "Let them take the animals. For each one they take I will get a hundred back."

DAVID GRIFFITHS was expelled from the Conservative Association in Twickenham, west London, after making a speech to an audience of two people in York House in August 1995. Among other outrageous views, he had urged that all criminals should be killed, all homosexuals should commit suicide and those claiming social security benefit should gun each other down in the street. He bounced back in January 1996 by announcing that he was standing as the Antichrist in the next General Election. Griffiths, 35, claimed to have known he was the Antichrist for some time, but kept it secret for fear it would damage his political career. His campaign for the Twickenham seat was being financed by a £37,000 legacy left in his parents' will. He circulated a 44-page manifesto in an attempt to woo voters, but sank without trace at the polls.

DAILY MAIL reader Mr Harold Ellis has the ultimate solution to football hooliganism. In a letter to the paper he expounded his philosophy. "They could be cured by being made to wear proper hats", he wrote. "Good behaviour has all but disappeared since men stopped wearing them."

I'M NOT SURE what Mr Ellis would have made of a man Hong Kong police stopped because he seemed "oddly shaped". On investigation they found he was wearing 18 bras and 45 pairs of ladies panties.

AN UNUSUAL CASE was highlighted by Dr Ranjani Pandita-Gunawardena in the British Journal of Psychiatry. One of his patients was a man who lived as a baby for 60 years. He slept in a huge cot, played with a teddy bear and ate baby food while sitting in a man-sized high chair. He was looked after by his sister who took him for walks in a specially-built pram. His strange lifestyle only came to light after he asked a neighbour to change his nappy. He was found not to be mentally ill and doctors respected his wish not to be cured of his strange fixation, until his death at the age of 80.

EVEN STRANGER, Barry Kirk lives his life as a baked bean. Kirk, 42, wears an orange jump-suit and cape and paints his bald head orange. He eats baked beans every day and takes baths in the food. He has changed his name by deed poll to Captain Beany and when he needed a passport to match his new identity he produced a completely orange photo of himself. "At last I can travel abroad under my real identity" he said. Passport official Malcolm Taylor commented "We were happy to deal with Captain Beany's request, even though his head is orange we were satisfied it was a good likeness." He did however add "There may be problems at frontier control."

RATHER than painting his head orange, Tatsumi Orimoto straps bread to it. He spent June 1996 wandering London's open spaces with baguettes tied to his head, following up the two years he spent in Germany walking round with a 9ft (2.7m) chimney in his backpack and the five years he'd spent crossing continental roads with a cardboard box on his foot. He'd also spent a year in New York dragging a cast iron bathtub round Greenwich Village. The Japanese artist, known as "Bread Head" said "It's my way of communicating."

IN JULY 1996 Peter Doden was walking his dog in Wakerley Woods, Northamptonshire, when the dog slipped its collar and dashed off. When he caught up, the dog was looking up into a tree and barking at an elderly gentleman sitting astride on e of the branches. "Good morning" ventured Doden. "Yes it is, it is," said the man. "Have you a spare sandwich or anything ?" Mr Doden threw him a chocolate bar which he devoured, wrapper and all, before revealing that he had been in the tree for a fortnight. "I set out to join those tree-sitters in Sussex protesting about a new road," he said, "but when I reached Wakerley Woods I felt rather tired and decided to lodge my protest in this tree instead." Mr Doden pointed out that Sussex was 150 miles (240km) to the south and that in any case the tree protesters there were long gone. "Damn it all," replied the elderly eco-warrior, "they might have told me."

MICHAEL BALAMA, a 45-year-old farmer and father of nine from the village of Mhweli on Nigeria, had a row with one of his two wives in 1987 and spent the following five years up a locust-bean tree. He only fell out once. His wives fed him by leaving meals on low branches. In February 1992 he came down, rowed with the other wife and ran away. After a search by neighbours, he was found up an olive tree on top of a mountain a kilometre from his house where he said he was "fine", but couldn't come down because of spirits. A healer, Doctor Kaya, hoped to appease the tree spirits with blood sacrifices. "There are evil spirits holding him from coming down from the tree, and until these spirits are appeased there is no hope of him coming down", he said.

IN SIKEBUT, Indonesia, a man named Kasbi, 34, has never forgiven himself for his meanness to his mother shortly before her death in 1972. Ever since he has been standing on the same spot, gazing out an empty rubber plantation in front of his house, attracting a crowd of onlookers every day.

AFTER HIS OWN death, comic book writer Mark Gruenwald's dying wish was to be thrown into the pages of his own work. Following a heart-attack on 12 August 1996 the ashes of the 43-year-old Marvel Comics writer and editor were mixed with ink and used to print the 12-part comic series "Squadron Supreme" as a 100-page volume. In January 1986 one man decreed in his will that his hearse should speed to the cemetery at more than 80mph, while Lewis Bush, who shot himself in a Swindon hospital at the age of 70, left instructions that he was to be cremated to the sound of a brass band playing "Wish me Luck as You Wave me Goodbye", and Eric Cramp, an 82-year-old retired steelworker shocked his former colleagues by leaving instructions that he should be buried in lace underwear, a cocktail dress and made up like a woman. He had hidden his longing to be a woman from them for years. In 1834, when John 'Mad Jack' Fuller died, he was buried in a pyramid in Brightling churchyard, Sussex, seated in an armchair holding a bottle of claret. Broken glass was scattered around him so that "when the Devil comes to claim his own he will at least cut his feet."

GEOFF SMITH planned to honour the memory of his mother, Emma, by spending six months 10ft (3m) underground in a steel coffin, beneath 100 tons of soil at Sun City, Skegness, Lincolnshire. At the same venue in 1968 Emma Smith had spent 101 days buried alive. Geoff was hoping to beat the 140 day record held by an American. Visitors would be able to see him through a hole in the top of the coffin. Food was to be passed in through a hatch in the top, and a second hatch opened into a septic tank underneath, for obvious reasons. "I've got a holiday to look forward to afterwards" said Mr Smith. "I promised to take my kids on a cruise."

CHAPTER FOUR

Dumb Or Dumber

Stupidity beyond the call of duty

AMONG the letters sent to a US medical foundation as entries to a competition offering free cryogenic preservation - body freezing - as a prize for the person giving the best reason for wanting it was one from a man who wanted to be frozen so he could have sex with aliens. He claimed to be fed up with ordinary women because they were "easy" and wanted the chance to bed a shapely extraterrestrial. Also trying for the prize were a failed comedian who hoped his jokes would go down better in the future and an aspiring serial killer who reasoned "since weapons of mass destruction will be more readily available in the future, I'd like to come back then so I can rack up a higher body count."

CHAPTER FOUR

IF HE DID get his wish, he would have done well to avoid the city of Chico in California. There it is an offence, carrying a fine of up to $500, to let off a nuclear weapon within the city limits. In Wyoming, the laws are even more draconian - it is illegal to photograph rabbits between the months of January and March without written permission anywhere in the state.

POLICE CALLED to a New Zealand house because a howling dog was upsetting neighbours found that the owners had gone away, leaving the dog behind. Sensitive to its welfare they had also left food in bowls labelled "Monday", "Tuesday", "Wednesday", "Thursday" etc. By Tuesday, however, the illiterate dog had scoffed the lot, then began howling for more.

TWO MEN who kidnapped a young circus lion and made off with it in the back of their car in Siracusa, Italy, were later found by police - dazed, covered in scratches and minus the lion.

DRUNKEN TRUCK DRIVER Brad Parker knew just what to do to foil the breathalyser when cops pulled him over in Illinois - he ripped open his trousers, tore off his underpants and ate them. He believed that the cotton would absorb the alcohol from his breath and allow him to escape scot free. It didn't.

AN ITALIAN motorist in Germany decided to test the limits of divine intervention while driving on the motorway. "I wanted to know, so I let go and asked 'God, can you drive?'" he told police. He clearly couldn't as the car immediately swerved off the road and crashed, although the driver was unhurt in the accident. German judges banned him from driving for 20 months.

STOPPED for driving too slow on the M25 in Kent a motorist surprised police by asking if he was near Durham yet. They told him that 10 hours after embarking on his journey he was in fact 20 miles further from his destination than when he started out, and was only a few miles from home. Travelling at about 25mph the man had driven anti-clockwise round the motorway before heading north on the M11. On reaching the A1 at Huntingdon, instead of turning north, he headed south, arriving back on the M25. He then continued round the London ring-road through Hertfordshire, Berkshire and Surrey, before the patrol car pulled him over in Swanley, 20 miles south of his starting point.

IN BOLIVIA a teenager jokingly glued a skittle to her forehead during a ten-pin-bowling match, then couldn't get it off, ending up in hospital so it could be detached surgically. In Akron, Ohio, a six-year-old boy took up a friend's dare to lick an iron fire-hydrant in freezing weather, only to find it stuck firmly. "He couldn't really talk when we got there, but he was crying pretty good." said paramedic Doug Fela. "Some bystanders had tried to pour water on his tongue, but that just made it worse." The paramedics released him with saline solution.

IT WAS HARDER for medics to free Peter Aupke, 29. He covered his penis in quick-drying cement so that he could make a mould to cast a rubber replica of his tackle for his wife. It needed the delicate intervention of a Munich surgeon to cut him free. Also in Germany, fireman freed an embarrassed 22-year-old's penis from the handle of a hollow hammer after it got stuck there during a bizarre sex experiment.

FOLLOWING the death of Paul Simone, 33, in a car crash, his best friend Henri Cousteau (also 33), of Marseilles, became the beneficiary of an unusual legacy. In his will Simone left Cousteau his 9.75 in (24cm) penis for transplantation. "I never had real sex" he said "Paul had hundreds of women. Now I could have the same success." Dream on Henri. Sharing Henri's dream was impotent Turk Mehmet Esirgen, 52, who was not willing just to sit around and wait for someone to give him a penis, he decided to go out and get one for himself. On three occasions he bought a donkey, amputated its sexual organs and appealed in vain for a doctor to perform the transplant. His third attempt so annoyed his family that Mehmet's son shot him in the leg. He intended to buy a fourth donkey when he got out of hospital. One man in Wuhu, eastern China, did not have much choice when it came to extending his penis. His wife cut it off while he slept in the belief that it would grow back bigger than before.

ARMANDO BOTALEZZI was rushed to hospital in Italy after trying to alter the shape of his nose with a pair of pliers. Botalezzi, 32, explained that he could not afford plastic surgery. Making a similar error was Carmen Ruiz, 62, from Barcelona. She tried smoothing out wrinkles on her neck and hands with a hot iron, landing herself in a burns unit for her trouble. But the most direct approach has to be that of a farmer from Sicuani, Peru. Wracked by toothache he tried to solve the problem by shooting the offending tooth out with a pistol. He succeeded... but blew most of his lower jaw away in the process.

EVEN IF people do opt for proper medical treatment, there's no guarantee their own stupidity won't intervene. In Turkey, doctors had to perform urgent surgery on Hasan Seker after nurses tried to take his temperature. He mistook the thermometer for medicine and swallowed it. In Norway a 69-year-old man recovering from heart surgery complained of abdominal pain. Diagnosing appendicitis doctors decided to operate, but when they got in there they found that his bowel had been perforated by the sharp corner of the blister wrap containing one of his pills. He hadn't been unwrapping them before swallowing.

MUSTAFA KAYA, a Turkish farmer, accidentally swallowed a fly. Having heard that flies were fast breeders, he immediately gulped down insecticide to kill it. "I never knew just a bit of insecticide could do me harm" he said from his hospital bed in the eastern town of Malatya.

BRUSH SALESMAN Dan Craig of Alberta, Canada, lost both his job and his wife when he admitted spending their £10,000 life savings on more than 5000 brushes to make his sales figures look better.

DOUG MERRILL failed in his attempt to sue an American electricity company for $500,000 damages. He brought the claim after he suffered serious burns while trying to cook an eel on one of their high-voltage power lines.

TWO PETROL station attendants in Eunice, Alabama handed over $350 to a naked man who marched into their garage and claimed to have a gun in his back pocket. In Michigan a bank clerk panicked when a beggar walked up to her counter and politely asked for 50 cents for a cup of coffee and handed over $5000. The beggar thanked her and strolled out. Arrested three days later he was found to have spent most of the money - but he wasn't charged. "There was no weapon or intimidation so he's got to go free" said a police spokesman "he told us he was real surprised when he got so much cash from the lady."

CHAPTER FOUR

THE THIRD Lord Leconfield, out fox-hunting during World War II, came across a village soccer match. Standing up in his stirrups, he shouted: "Haven't you people got anything better to do in wartime than play football?"

DURING the Cold War two CIA agent Weatherby and Corbin, were exposed after trying to conceal electronic sensing and broadcasting devices inside an artificial tree stump to spy on a Soviet defence installation. They were let down by their ignorance of Russian flora: their fake pine stump was put in a grove of aspen trees.

A TEACHER at a middle school in Marepas, west of Paris, caused astonishment by setting her physics pupils the following question: "Hitler killed Jews by locking them in trucks whose exhaust pipe was connected to the inside. Knowing the volume of a bus is 50 cubic metres, what volume of carbon monoxide must be given off to attain the mortal dose of five parts per 1,000? Knowing the victims took 20 minutes to die on average, what volume of carbon monoxide was produced hourly by the engine?"

ALFONSO NINO, 75, a retired Navy pilot from Nipomo, California, who is listed in the phone book as Al Nino, has had more than 100 calls from people blaming him for the El Nino storms. One caller told him he was responsible for his daughter losing her virginity. She had been unable to get home after a storm blocked the road and had spent the night in the car with her boyfriend.

CHAPTER FIVE

Conspicuous Consumption

Never mind the old joke about the "See-Food Diet" - these people were on a "See-Anything Diet"

OBESE THAI Chote Ontrakran's finally lost control of his stuffing urge and tried to eat his home in Lop Buri. 24st 4lb Chote attempted to scoff the entire contents of his lounge. Over a 7 month period he managed to eat most of the furniture, his TV and the stereo. Incredibly, he survived his bizarre meal and relatives found him writhing with indigestion on what was left of his carpet.

CHOTE MIGHT have benefited from a treatment developed by the Yan Hee Polyclinic in Bangkok. They recommend sticking lettuce seeds in your ears to help you lose weight.

According to the clinic, pressing the seeds in your ears 10 times before meals will kill hunger.

POLLY GRABOWITZ, 36, suffered unfortunate consequences from her addiction to sherbert. Eating 5lbs of the sweet a day made her so bloated with wind that she got stuck in the swing doors of the local candy store in Memphis, Tennessee and had to be freed by four firemen. In Hobart, Tasmania, the local paper reported the case of one un-named woman who had to keep running out of her shop when flatulence was about to strike, often joined by many of her neighbours. "People often think we go outside together to puff on cigarettes" she said "In fact, we go out to fart - it might sound funny, but it's not." Michael Cook of the Australian Medical Association doubted the rumour that the farting epidemic was caused by viruses, but said "I'll certainly be keeping my ears open for sounds of mass farting ...and see if any of my colleagues are being deafened by this so called epidemic."

A MAN dubbed "The Human Engine" became notorious in Reading,, Berkshire for walking into his local petrol station and drinking the dregs from the four-star nozzles - then paying the cashier 2p. Asked why he did it, he told staff at the Weldale garage "It's good for me", but Berkshire health chiefs weren't so sure. "He has to excrete this petrol somehow, so he must be a fire risk" they warned.

FAR MORE DANGEROUS is the habit of an Iranian girl named Sahar - she is addicted to cooking gas. The 14-year-old gas huffer began her habit as a child according to her mother "She was so fond of aerosols in her childhood and used to breath in their contents. At the age of five , she screamed unless she was allowed to open the gas pressure container and make use of that.

When she was seven, she used to loiter in the kitchen, and as soon as I left, even for a second, I would small gas and catch her breathing it from the stove. We tried all sorts of things to stop her, but it was no use." Sahar is small, but very strong and a great acrobat with a talent for climbing and picking locks. Unlike most teenagers she does not watch TV, but instead prefers to stand on the highest point of the building. Her mother said "No one can go near her because she stinks of gas. When others try to stop her, she eats inflammable glue." Doctors examining her found she had an IQ of around 60, drastically lowered by her addiction. They said she was physically fit, but recommended keeping her away from heat in case of explosions.

ALSO IN IRAN 70-year-old Mr Darvish from Tehran amazed doctors by drinking a bottle of industrial alcohol every day for 20 years. Highly poisonous, it usually blinds people by destroying the nerves in their eyes, gives them brain damage and wrecks their livers, but it seems to have no effect on Darvish. Asked why he drank it, he said "because I want to stay sober". He doesn't drink ordinary alcohol and after his chosen tipple, eats a sugar lump to clear his palate. He believes that if you have a free mind, you will live a long life and thinks he will survive to be 125.

IN IRELAND in the late 19th century ether drinking was widespread, with one contemporary report estimating that one in eight of the population at the time were ether addicts. Ether vaporises at body temperature so drinkers had to develop a ritual to overcome this. They would rinse out their mouth with cold water, hold the nose and swallow the ether, quickly followed by more cold water. Regular etheromaniacs could sink a pint of the stuff a day in this way. If they failed to "rift" (belch) at the appropriate moment, explosive vaporisation could cause a heart attack, and there were cases when people rifting near naked flames had fire travel down their throats causing them to explode.

LIQUID NITROGEN has a temperature of -196 degrees centigrade, so playing with it was probably not the best idea a Massachusetts postgrad ever had. Reminded of an old party trick by the behaviour of nitrogen droplets skittering around a table on a layer of vaporising gas, he decided to show how the same phenomenon allowed you to drink the stuff . "So, I poured myself a glass and took a shot. Simple. Swallow. Blow smoke out nose and mouth and impress everyone at the party." he said. However " Within about two seconds, I had collapsed to the floor, unable to breathe or feel anything other than intense pain. Wake up next morning connected to many machines, some beeping, others performing more important functions like digesting my food and breathing for me." He had found out the hard way that, in accordance with popular belief, you really should not drink the stuff. What had happened was that when he swallowed, the closing of the epiglottis prevented the expanding nitrogen gas from escaping, so it was forced into his body instead. In addition, your oesophagus naturally constricts around anything inside it, so, even if there is a thin protective gas layer, the oesophagus will find a way to make contact with the liquid nitrogen, resulting in extensive tissue damage. His entire upper digestive tract, from the epiglottis to the bottom of the stomach was badly burned, scarred, and perforated. The gas also expanded quite a bit while inside his body, filling his chest cavity with several litres of nitrogen gas, which was under enough pressure to collapse a lung. Surgeons had to remove part of his stomach, put his entire digestive system on life support for several days, as well as put him on a breathing machine until his lungs were able to work again. He recovered with impressive scarring, the first recorded victim of cryogenic ingestion.

POLICE in Cheltenham, Gloucestershire, were on the track of an unusual burglar who broke into five homes in one night. Taking only trivial items, his main target seemed to be the fridge. In every house he raided, he broke into it and drank all the milk. He might have done well to team up with an unnamed Canadian whose habit was reported in the medical journal The Lancet. Apparently he filled his bath with hot water, added hundreds of teabags, then sat in it, drinking the tea by dipping a mug in it. According to the report "He considered it only to be an enjoyable experience in a very large teapot."

IT'S NOT JUST alcoholic drinks which can be addictive, Christopher Maynard, 30, from New Milton, Hampshire, had to be hospitalised to cure his Coke addiction. He needed to drink five cans just to stop shaking in the morning and downed 40 in the course of an average day. "In a bad month I once drank over 2,200 cans of Coke" he said "I only get £26 a week social security, but as I spend over £70 a week on Coke I have been forced to sell everything I own except the dog." He tried to compensate for this by building a replacement three-piece-suite out of empty Coke tins. For Kevin Simpkin, 27, it was Snapple that did the trick - he lost his job as a Snapple delivery driver after being caught drinking his cargo instead of delivering it, then got arrested for swiping a Snapple truck while dressed in a uniform he'd kept. "He just has an uncontrollable urge for Snapple beverages" said arresting officer Det.Lieut August Grenier, "he even had a Snapple T-shirt depicting a bottle of iced tea under his uniform. He just loves Snapple."

INGRID SMITH suffered from an uncontrollable craving for water, she was downing 18 pints a day and had put on 12 stone in a year. Former water addict Joy Gray told her "It can be beaten" she had been drinking three gallons a day at one point, but had fought the compulsion with diet Coke - 50 cans a week, reducing her weight to 13.5 stone. Less lucky was Toothache sufferer Tom Nield. Over a long weekend, with all dentists closed, Nield found that the only way to dull the raging pain was by drinking chilled water - 20 gallons of it, equivalent to a bathful. The huge amount of water diluted his blood so much that he collapsed in a coma and had to be rushed to a Glasgow hospital. Coming to three days later he vowed "I'm sticking to real drink".

AN ISRAELI medical student horrified university authorities in Jerusalem by eating a human brain to win a £10 bet. She was immediately suspended while an investigation into the incident was carried out.

WES HASTINGS of Nevada became a cigarette addict after being dared to smoke one by a friend. Unlike most fag fiends however, Hastings ate his and now scoffs 60 a day, usually in a buttered sandwich with a touch of salt and mustard.

HEALTH AUTHORITIES in Taiyuan, central China discovered a woman in her mid-30s who enjoyed the taste of rubber so much she had eaten over 800 rubber nipples from baby bottles over a three-year period. The Economic Evening News added "It's said all the woman's family like the smell of rubber, and her younger brother is fond of eating rubber bands."

CHICAGO RESEARCHERS scoured medical literature for cases of people who had swallowed their toothbrushes, finding 31 cases in all. Four of the incidents occurred in Durham, North Carolina. Two of the Carolina swallowers had apparently drunk a large quantity of alcohol, while a third was a 60-year-old who had a seizure while brushing her teeth. She complained only of throat pain but examination revealed the brush stuck in her throat - it was removed with forceps. The fourth was a 20-year-old woman who developed a violent coughing fit while scrubbing and swallowed her brush. It made its way down to her stomach and surgeons snared it with a wire dropped down through her mouth. Despite the Durham cluster they said "this problem should probably not be considered endemic to North Carolina" pointing out that one region in India reported six swallowings between 1960 and 1973, while the champion swallower was a Soviet psychiatric patient who swallowed 16 toothbrushes in 1984.

TURKISH POLICE were hunting a woman who raids flower shops and flees after eating the heads off roses. Shortly afterwards a man was undergoing psychiatric tests in Bangkok after breaking into a model's home and eating nine silk dresses.

DRUG ADDICTS in Kuala Lumpur, Malaysia dealt with a shortage of cocaine and cannabis by developing a new vice - dung sniffing. "They will wait for the fresh cow dung and quickly put a coconut shell over it, then sniff the gas through the hole in the top of the shell," Deputy Home Minister Megat Junid Ayob told a drugs conference. In Dubai teenagers dealt with a similar shortage by turning to ants. They were smoking the insects or sniffing the fumes they emitted when crushed. Police had arrested a number of youths who had become intoxicated in this way and said a new drug trade was underway with a small packet of "Samaseem" - Gulf Arabic for ants- selling for $135.

IN CALCUTTA, the city's poorer drug addicts have also found a cheap replacement for heroin and cocaine - lizard tails. They make the reptile appendages into a powder by grinding and roasting them. The powder is then rolled into cigarettes, with an average-sized tail good for two smokes. The habit began in Calcutta following reports of habitual use by a Manipur tribe.

MALAYSIAN DOCTORS suspected a man of swallowing heroin-filled condoms, but discovered he had actually eaten several iguana eggs whole. After eating S.Adinrayanan suffered pains and had to have the eggs surgically removed. Ernesto Mota actually did swallow bags of drugs - he swallowed a bag of cocaine to avoid having it used as evidence against him, giving himself internal injuries in the process. He then tried to sue Illinois police for £4million for making him do it.

ACCORDING TO the Eastern Express newspaper in Hong Kong there is foetus eating fad in the Chinese city of Shenzen. An investigating reporter apparently visited the Shenzen Centre for Women and Children and asked a female doctor for a foetus. The next day she allegedly gave him "a fist sized glass bottle stuffed with thumb-sized foetuses" saying "There are ten foetuses here, all aborted this morning. You can take them". They were claimed to be "nutritious" when eaten as a soup, together with pork, orange peel and ginger. They were supposed to "..make your skin smoother, your body stronger and be good for your kidneys."

A WOMAN in Memphis, Tennessee, sued a small pharmacy because she bought a tube of contraceptive jelly, spread it on toast and ate it. She then had unprotected sex, believing she was "safe" and became pregnant. She was asking for half a million dollars, even though she was quoted as saying: "Who has time to sit around reading directions these days, especially when you're sexually aroused?"

CHAPTER SIX

Take That!

People seem to have an infinite capacity for violence, and are endlessly inventive with it

WHEN STEVEN VERNON, a shoe salesman from Brownsville, Texas, forgot his girlfriend's birthday, she decided to get even. Furious Patty Fouch went to the local pet shop and bought a dozen razor-toothed piranha fish, cut a hole in Vernon's water bed and slipped the savage critters inside, sealing the gash with tape. The first her boyfriend knew of it was when the frenzied fish gnawed through the plastic and sank their teeth painfully into his backside.

FURIOUS BRIDEGROOM Erik Bentsen, 35, sued his pals after they pounced on him on his stag night and daubed his wedding tackle with luminous paint which he couldn't remove. He claimed his penis glowed in the dark, putting him and his new bride off of sex, ruining their honeymoon. "I thought they were my friends but no true pal would paint your privates the night before your wedding." said Erik "I now want to teach them a lesson."

IN PETERBOROUGH, Cambridgeshire, ambulance men came under a novel form of attack when called to deal with a deranged man going berserk with a kitchen knife - he cut off his penis and hurled it at them to try and fend them off. In Jakarta, police arrested a man believed to have bitten off the penises of "at least five" young schoolboys after a two-year hunt. Dressed as a woman, the man was captured at a bus terminal "after he bit the penis of a bus conductor he mistook for a prostitute."

IN JAMAICA puzzled police were on the track of a mugger who beat people up, then stuffed £30 into their pockets before running away, while in Stockholm cops were puzzled by a weirdo in a gorilla suit who was stalking the city, pouncing on unsuspecting women.

ALSO THE VICTIM of a costumed assailant was former Chicago Bulls cheerleader Kimberly Smith, who was injured when a man dressed as a chicken forced her to dance with him. The Famous Chicken - also known as Ted Giannoulas - who performs at US sports events apparently forced her into a quick dance then rolled on her on the floor.

IN AUSTIN, Texas, Roland Wood was attacked by a man armed with a bat who leapt out of the shadows and struck him on the shoulder with it. Uninjured, but startled and offended, he called the police. When they arrived they quickly detained a man and searched him, looking for a baseball bat. The suspect said it was in his backpack, but police couldn't find it, so he pulled it out - not a baseball bat, but a Mexican Freetail Bat, one of a colony of 1.5 million which roost in the city. Surprised, the police made him turn the creature loose and filed an assault charge. While they could remember no other assaults using a live bat as a weapon they stated emphatically "It's against the law to chuck bats at people."

NEW ZEALAND poultry worker Norman Hireme was fined $50 after being found guilty of causing a chicken extreme pain and distress - during an argument at work he grabbed a bird off the production line, pointed it at his colleague and squeezed it so violently that excrement shot several metres hosing the man. He repeated this several times before replacing the chicken on the conveyor to be electrically stunned and slaughtered.

BIG DOGS are often seen as more dangerous than small ones, but it depends how you use them - Debby Wiggs of Oklahoma ended up adding animal cruelty charges to those of assault and drunk driving after she beat a traffic cop round the head with her pet dog when he pulled her over, while in Fillmore, California a 13-year-old boy was arrested for hurling a Chihuahua at his mother during a violent argument. "I have never seen a Chihuahua assault in my 26 years of law enforcement and I'll probably not see it again" said arresting officer Lt. Gary Markey.

IN SAO PAULO a raider robbed a restaurant armed with a giant cockroach - he thrust the insect into the cashiers face, then grabbed £200 from the till when she fled into the kitchen. In Geraldton, Western Australia, a shop raider dealt with the cashier by super-glueing her head to the counter while he rifled the till, while in Wolverhampton, muggers pounced on John

Parsons in a lift and incapacitated him by dragging him to a boiler room and nailing his hand to a piece of wood. They turned his pockets out and escaped with 40p.

THE FBI were on the track of a Florida bank robber who didn't need to carry a weapon. Dubbed "Mr Stinky" or "The B.O. Bandit" his body odour was so repulsive bank tellers were willing to do what he said just to get away from the stench.

AFTER REFUSING to give a man a cigarette while walking along Wheelwright Road, Erdington, Lancashire, a 27-year-old man was beaten and badly bruised with a tyre. Elsewhere, in Fort Smith, Arkansas, Garry Campbell, 41, ended up in hospital in a serious condition after three fellow homeless men beat him senseless with a porcelain toilet tank to stop him snoring. They also shaved his head.

ALSO in the head-shaving game was an armed pervert hunted by police in Genoa, Italy. He held 24 women at gunpoint and forced them to shave their heads. High school soccer coach Jesus Valencia Gomez, 45, was arrested in Whittier, California, for practising medicine without a licence. He had told a 24-year-old woman she had cancerous tumours on her neck and head and would need surgery. He anaesthetised her, shaved her head and bandaged her in a motel room. The woman only notified authorities several days later, when she discovered that she had no scar under the bandages.

IN the Partile area of Goteborg, Sweden, young women were terrorised by a very large person, dressed as a woman, but thought to be a man, who was cutting hair from their heads, then running away. The press called him the "Sax Maniac", "Sax" being Swedish for "pair of scissors". He only struck late at night on holidays. In Grosse Point Woods, Michigan, four women reported a man for fondling their hair while watching the film Sleepless in Seattle at the cinema. At least two of the victims believed the man may have been sucking their hair - they found it was wet. In Baton Rouge, Louisiana, police charged Redmomd McGee, 25, with breaking into a woman's house and brushing her hair against her will.

FAST FOOD COOK George Kuehme, 20, was sentenced to 45 days in jail for aggravated assault after he blew his nose on a police officer's hamburger in Phoenix, Arizona, while in Kansas City Milton Ross exacted an even more hideous revenge on his feuding co-workers. He was fired when a video trap, set after they noticed their coffee tasting sour, caught him urinating in the coffee pot before other staff arrived at work. The ultimate, though, must be Missouri chemical plant janitor, Terrence Sellers. Upset after his work was criticised, he spiked his supervisor's diet soda with a radioactive isotope.

VICTORIAN PRIME-MINISTER Gladstone was the victim of a bizarre assault in his old age. Blind in one eye, he suffered the misfortune of having his good eye seriously injured by a piece of gingerbread flung "with great force and skill" by "a middle aged bony woman". Although this is one of the earliest recorded food attacks, it is far from the last, Jilted lover David Fricker, 44, was arrested for assaulting his old flame Linda Knowles with a frozen Gateau in Mold, North Wales, and in Lincoln, police were pursuing a cyclist who hurled a Mars bar at a woman walking beside the river Witham. In Reading, Richard Eastwood, 26, had an assault charge dropped by magistrates when he appeared in court accused of hitting a pedestrian with an extra strong mint flicked out of a car, but in Borneo Dayu Kalim got 10 years in prison for throwing a coconut at a sword swallower in mid-swallow. The man's career was ruined.

APPROPRIATELY named Mohammed Jabber, 33, was jailed for three years for kidnapping a former Bangladeshi politician in Poplar, east London and jabbing a chilli pepper up his rectum in an argument over debt. Jabber, a community worker, photographed the man as he suffered "considerable pain".

IN BIDDEFORD, Maine, police arrested two men after a drive-by pastrying. Laurie Remillard was walking through the town early one Sunday when she was hit in the face with a salvo of doughnut holes flung from a passing car. She got the number and police grabbed Chris Roy, 19 and Christopher Cote, 20, for the crime. They admitted they were no strangers to doughnut flinging, but usually attacked street signs and were not sure why they had chosen a human victim on this occasion.

ALSO HAVING TROUBLE coming up with an explanation was Robert Jones of Sydney, Australia. After he was arrested for pulling a Koala from a tree on a golf course, kicking it, stabbing it five times in the neck, decapitating it and drinking its blood, police asked him why he did it, he said it was hard to explain. His friends said he was a kind and gentle man and his behaviour came as a complete surprise to them. The judge released him on a three-year good behaviour bond, but said it was "regrettable that the matter proceeded to trial during National Koala Week."

ERIK AND KARL LUDOLTER were arrested after exchanging violent blows with each other during a brawl in Capetown, South Africa. The siamese twins, who are joined at the chest, fell out when Karl blamed Erik for drinking too much and resorted to fisticuffs, leaving him nursing a bruised face.

POLICE in Sidmouth, Devon, tracked down Tim Farndon, 38, after a man reported seeing him attacking himself with a hammer. It turned out that Farndon experienced violent headaches after a car crash 20 years before had resulted in a blocked brain duct and the only way to cure them was to beat himself about the head with a rubber mallet.

POSSIBLY the most baffling fight ever occurred between Brother Fernand Bremaud, 71, and Brother Eric Metivier, 28, Trappist monks in a monastery in Holland, Manitoba. Brother Fernand ended up in hospital with stab wounds and Brother Metivier down the police station on assault charges. It is baffling because Trappists are a silent order, forbidden to speak, making one wonder how such an acrimonious fight could actually begin.

IN 1986 American TV anchorman Dan Rather was leapt on by a mysterious assailant who knocked him to the ground and kicked him several times, all the while demanding "Kenneth, what is the frequency?", a bizarre occurrence which inspired the REM song "What's the frequency, Kenneth?". Eleven years later the mystery was solved when William Tager, in prison for murder, was identified by Rather as his assailant. Apparently Tager was convinced the media had him under surveillance and were beaming hostile messages at him. He ran into Rather by chance while in New York under the impression he had an appointment with a female TV personality to discuss ending the messages. He thought he had been stood up when he saw Rather and decided to beat the frequency they were using to make the hostile broadcasts out of him. But why Kenneth ?

A WOMAN from South Wales, sunbathing on the cliffs in the centre of Newquay, Cornwall, complained to two men that they were playing football too close to her. The men rushed towards her, snapped a lock round her ankle to which was attached a heavy ball and chain, and ran off. It had to be removed by the fire brigade, using crash-rescue equipment and cutting gear. Police in Winchester, meanwhile were after a 6ft man in his forties who rushed up to women, yelled: "Beep, Beep!", molested them as they shrieked and ran off laughing. In Digbeth, Birmingham, a woman traffic warden was walking to work when a man leapt in front of her, smeared her face with toothpaste from a piece of cardboard and fled.

SOMEONE in Sandusky, Illinois, was preying on Barbie Dolls. He ripped their clothes off and slashed them across the breasts and crotch with a knife. More than 24 dolls were attacked. Grant Oliver, 25, a carpenter from Torquay, was arrested in the early hours after a stag night party when police saw him punching and shouting abuse at a life-size rubber doll. He was locked up for the night, and fined £80 for threatening behaviour likely to cause harassment, alarm or distress.

CHAPTER SEVEN

Insane Clown Posse

Clowns are supposed to be *funny* … but sometimes you really wonder

IN ASPEN, Colorado, city officials staged a crackdown on the city's clowns. A group of local mothers complained to the Commercial Core and Lodging Commission that some summer street performers weren't conducting themselves properly and should by subject to supervision. The mothers said that some clowns used lewd language and had holes in their pants in inappropriate places.

ANIMAL RIGHTS CAMPAIGNERS protesting outside a circus complained to police after they were beaten up by clowns. They claimed they were set upon by a pack of clowns as they protested outside Miller's Circus in Bursledon, near Southampton, Hants. One woman suffered a broken cheekbone and four others were injured when the protest ended in violence.

IN NEW YORK a 12-year-old Hispanic boy was attacked and beaten up in 1992 by unknown individuals who completed the assault by painting the child's face with white clowns make up. It was the second such incident within a week.

IN ROUGHAM, Suffolk, two young children ran screaming to their mother after a boy dressed as a clown threw a stone through the window of the car in which they were waiting for her. Mrs Georgina Barefield was shopping in Rougham post office, leaving six-year-old Carl and Lisa, four outside with their dog in her Vauxhall Nova when the clown struck. The stone smashed the rear passenger window of the car spraying the inside with glass which narrowly missed Carl. The boy, believed to be in his teens then reached into the car to retrieve the stone before fleeing.

NEWLYWED Daniel Barrat took his wife to a circus in Australia as a honeymoon treat - but she ran off with one of the clowns. Dominique, 22, fell for Bucky the clown after she volunteered to help him with one of his stunts. In Ogden, Utah, though, a mechanic living in a mobile home answered a knock at his door to be confronted by a clown with purple hair and makeup wearing bedroom slippers. The clown said he was looking for "Kathy" and accused the mechanic of having an affair with her. The mechanic denied knowing Kathy, whereupon the clown forced his way in, seized a lamp and hit the occupant over the head before fleeing.

IN PALM BEACH, Florida, a gunman dressed as a clown knocked on the door of mother-of-two Marlene Warren, 40, handed her balloons and flowers - then shot her in the head. Mrs Warren lay critically ill in hospital as mystified police hunted for the clown - and a motive. In Van Wert, Ohio, in the meantime, LeRoy Hullinger, 52, known to local children as Buttons the clown pleaded guilty to hiring a hit man to kill his wife in exchange for a microwave oven.

ON 4 OCTOBER 1995 a man dressed in a red nose, wig and fake Dracula teeth convinced nurses that he was delivering a get-well telegram to a male patient. He found the patient, produced a sawn-off shotgun and shot him. Fortunately the wound wasn't fatal as the victim turned away and took the force of the blast in his shoulder.

PLAYSCHEME CLOWN Gerald McDaniel, 23, an ex-drug addict, begged a court not to send him to jail for stealing three blouses from British Home Stores in Princes Street Edinburgh and giving police a false name and address, as the playscheme were keeping his job open for him. In Brighton however, a man about to give evidence to the county court in a squatting prosecution was dismissed for wearing a battery operated flashing red clowns nose.

A BIZARRE farmyard fight was quelled by the arrival of a clown in Woodcote, Oxfordshire. After an eight-year feud Donald Green, 59, screeched up to Ronald Booker's farmhouse and accused him of scratching his prized BMW. A struggle broke out and Booker, who had just been boozing down his local was knocked out, apparently during a struggle in which the pair wrestled with a pitchfork. Then Booker's fifteen-stone wife arrived on the scene and leapt on Green, knocked him flat, then sat on his face, forcing him to bite her bum to get free. Finally neighbour Susan Bartholomew arrived on the scene returning from a fancy dress party clad in a clown costume, she calmed everyone down, tying Green to a fence to prevent him pitching in again until police arrived. In court the Bookers and Green were bound over, and the court chairman Sid Lewington described the fracas as “extraordinary”.

POLICE were hunting a prankster dressed in a Halloween costume who had been terrifying old folks. Clad in black hooded robes and brandishing a scythe, he looked exactly like the classic image of Death incarnate. He was seen creeping up to windows in nursing homes and hospitals - terrifying elderly victims who believe the Reaper has arrived to end their lives. One ambushed pensioner said angrily “I was terrified. I just couldn’t move. I was so scared.” In a six month period he struck more than 50 times in Los Angeles, California. A policeman said “It might sound funny, but what this clown is doing is an invasion of privacy and that’s against the law.”

IN BASLE Switzerland, police had more trouble with a costumed character. A man dressed as Father Christmas was shot and wounded by cops after he bungled a burglary and took a woman hostage. He rang the doorbell of a house in one of the city’s residential areas, then threatened the young woman who opened the door with her small child. Her husband, hearing the commotion, escaped and raised the alarm.

IN 1994 Guatemala was gripped by a panic that North American tourists were kidnapping children and killing them to provide organs for the transplant trade. In April a man in clown makeup robbed a bus and soon the tourists were joined in the popular imagination by “bandit-clowns” intent on seizing their young. Clown-napper panics spread to the US as well that year with nearly 100 reports of sinister clowns being made in south-east Washington and Alexandria, Virginia. They began when an adolescent girl claimed a black man in his 20's, dressed in a red wig and nose, tried to lure her into a white 1993 ford van with Maryland plates by offering her sweets. When he didn't produce any, the girl bolted. The police regarded most of the subsequent sightings as bogus, saying "Any time people see a white van, they see a clown too." but in the ensuing weeks the firms of Fonzie the Clown and Balloons inc received 15 cancellations from parents who didn't want clowns at their children's parties.

A GROUP of clowns enticed and drove away 70 children aged three to six from schools and kindergartens in Oude Pekela in Holland near the German border. They were too scared to talk when they returned, but one mother found her daughter's body covered in cigarette burns. Police feared the children's ordeals may have been filmed for porn movies: some of the children said "We've been on TV."

IN CAPITAL HEIGHTS, Maryland, two men dressed in bushy wigs and red clown noses climbed into the car of a 54-year-old woman at a traffic intersection. They pulled guns on her and forced her to drive to the local Pepsi bottling plant, where they blindfolded her and placed her in the boot. She was then driven elsewhere, led into a room and cut in the shoulder and stomach before being released.

IN KAMPALA, Uganda, a maniac who was knocking out wild gorillas with tranquilliser darts, then dressing them in clown suits while unconscious was being hunted by police.

IN FAIRFAX County, Virginia, a young couple parked in a wood were astonished when their idyll was disturbed by the sight of an obviously angry man in a bunny-suit hacking at their windows with a hatchet. It was believed the man was protesting about new housing developments in the area as a couple of weeks later a security guard discovered him chopping at a porch post on one of the unfinished houses. "You are trespassing, " he announced to the startled guard. "If you come any nearer I'll chop your head off." then he bounded back into the woods. He was last seen by three children in Seat Pleasant, Maryland, on their way home from school, who told of seeing a man on the street "with his bunny suit on, with a hatchet."

BOB BRIGGS, 24, owner of a Domino's Pizza restaurant in Independence, Missouri, dressed as a giant red rabbit and stood in the road to attract business. He was knocked unconscious by Bobo the clown, who was promoting a Pizza Hut across the road. Briggs declined to press charges.

CHAPTER EIGHT

Smash It Up!

Even vandals can be strangely creative at times

A WOMAN in Bury St Edmunds, Suffolk was incredulous when she woke up one morning in 1994 and looked out at her prized 21-year-old Ford Escort. She had trouble getting the police to believe her when she rang up and told them "For some reason someone has completely wallpapered my car." But after they had been round, amazed officers launched a hunt for the DIY culprits. "We haven't got a clue why anyone would want to do this. We have never had a case like it before," they said. "You could say they can expect a pasting when we catch up with them!"

ALSO in a decorative mood were the vandals who broke into a park in Evesham, Worcestershire and painted two Vietnamese Pot-bellied Pigs completely gold.

ANOTHER PAINTER was exercising the skills of police in Darmstadt, Germany. They were questioning all the women in the town named Renate in an attempt to solve a curious case of vandalism. Someone had gone on the rampage in the town centre, spraying over 100 buildings with the words "I love Renate".

MARK JACKSON, from New York, probably regretted boasting about his fancy new toilet. On five separate occasions an intruder broke in and smashed it up. Police suspected a jealous neighbour.

LUCIA R., a 64-year-old Dutch woman known as the "furniture terrorist", was jailed for eight months for slashing sofas in furniture showrooms with a razor blade. Over six years she had caused damage of £300,000, cycling to shops in south Holland and north Belgium, ripping open cushions and carving on table tops.

IN SIX MONTHS, Delbridges Florists in Bedford Place, Southampton, had 1,000 carnation blooms plucked, leaving empty stalks. Nothing else was taken. After the enigmatic raids began, the florist Margaret Bagguley changed the locks, added extra bolts and a super-secure padlock, all to no avail. She sprinkled talcum powder on the floor - but no footprints were left. She tied a thread across the entrance-but it was never broken. She even hid the carnations - but they were always found. At the beginning only a few blooms were plucked in the night every now and then. Then the raids became more frequent, later the shop was raided three times in a week, with 165 blooms vanishing on the third occasion. The police made a thorough inspection of the shop, even checking the suspended ceiling, then made their deduction. "It must be a poltergeist" said PC Colclough, who headed the investigation.

IN PECKHAM, south London, police were completely without suspects in the case of the Phantom Wall Smasher. The rubble-making vandal struck 18 times in two months, destroying walls without leaving a trace. Police admitted they were baffled, "It's really weird" said investigating officer PC Terry Nicholls "One man heard a bang and saw bricks settling in a cloud of dust. But there was no-one around." The Phantom smashed one wall in half, tore a slab from another, knocked the top off a new wall and shattered canopies and pillars. "I'm going on holiday this weekend" said PC Nicholls wearily. "I dread to think what I'll find when I get back."

MANAGERS of the Hilltop Steak House were also baffled as to why anyone would want to cut the heads off its trademark herd of lifesize fake cows. Vandals apparently used power saws to decapitate six of the seven fibreglass cows outside the restaurant, and made off with a calf, cutting it off at the hoofs. "Nobody has called up claiming responsibility - no radical vegetarians," said assistant manager Marion Burke, "we have no idea why anyone would do it. I think it's just a college prank."

IN ROATH, Cardiff, police were on the track of a woman who sneaked into Catholic churches in the area and savagely smashed the heads off statues of the infant Jesus. In every case the baby had its head destroyed while the Madonna remained untouched. A church spokesman said "This woman could have a mental problem about children". Meanwhile, in Germany, Berlin police were hunting an axeman chopped the heads off 300 garden gnomes throughout the city.

HE WOULD have met his match with the fairy who went on the rampage in Rhos in Wales. On New Year's Eve 1991 a man dressed in a fairy costume wrenched a litter bin from the ground outside the Rhos Chippy in Church Street and hurled it through the door. He fled before police arrived. Shop owner Julian Socha said: "When I heard the news I thought it was someone who was disappointed we did not open on New Year's Eve, but on second thoughts none of our customers are fairies."

GARDENER Stephen Rushton looked out one morning and saw that his newly-laid lawn was still in perfect condition, except it was not where he had left it - it had moved 15 feet into the road outside his home. Overnight someone had rolled up the fresh turf and re-laid it as Rushton and his wife Jo slept. Car worker Stephen, 36, from Carterton, Oxfordshire, said "Apart from the fact that it was in the wrong place, they'd actually made quite a good job of it...it was laid along the road in neat rows. They must have spent ages doing it. I had to smile at first, but soon I got angry." Thirty other gardens on the estate were also vandalised the same night.

FURTHER Horticultural horrors were visited on Golden Gate Park in San Francisco by a man park gardeners dubbed "Johnny Weedseed". The mysterious character had been planting bits of South African Capeweed in the park's carefully tended lawns. Capeweed is a gardener's worst nightmare - an incredibly tenacious gruondcover plant which swarms all over an area, strangling any other plant in its path. "The only thing that really controls it is concrete," said Jim Rogers, assistant superintendent of the park. "No matter what you do, it just takes over." Gardeners managed to stop the man for long enough on one occasion to discover he was a German named Klaus, but then he got away. Describing Klaus' behaviour Rogers said "It's not exactly like a kid vandalising a tree or something, he takes weed cuttings from his knapsack and meticulously gives them a new home in the park." The only way park staff coped with the invasion was to dig up large plots of grass and replant it, as the thing is almost impervious to herbicides. Over three years Klaus managed to plant Capeweed in virtually every corner of the park. "I'm not sure if he doesn't know the trouble he's causing or he knows it very well," commented Rogers ruefully.

OTHER MUNICIPAL facilities also bear the brunt of vandals, with libraries apparently at the forefront. In Northampton, library staff were hunting a spoilsport who was working through the thriller section, ripping the final page out of all the whodunit books to frustrate readers, while in Cardiff bookshops another page-ripper was secretly tearing leaves in the middle of books then replacing them on shelves. Unsuspecting customers did not discover the books were ruined until they reached the damaged page. In every case half a page of text was neatly removed, always from hardbacks, but the subject could be anything from novels to manuals. The vandal kept it up for more than six months, but store owners remained baffled by the motive.

LONG BUCKBY library, near Daventry, Northants, was plagued by a sensitive and prudish vandal. They were working their way through all the best sellers in the building, eradicating all the swear words with a thick black marker pen. A spokesman said "The words are crossed out all the way through the books so somebody must have read them to the end to be able to do that.". A borrower commented "No one has the right to deface these books. If people do not like swear words they should chose different books to read instead of spoiling the copies for everybody else."

FARMER Dave Cannon was not bothered with books, but none the less was considerably concerned with filth. Frustrated by the council's fourth rejection of his plans to build a retirement home on his farm he loaded up a trailer with liquid manure and hosed council offices with four tonnes of the stuff. Unfortunately he directed the torrent of ordure at the wrong building, plastering the walls of the housing office with the stuff, leaving the place surrounded by a 10ft dung moat, while his real targets, planning officers, looked on with amazement from across the road. Not that this overly concerned the triumphant farmer "I feel good, even if it costs a few hundred, it was worth it... you have to prove your point, if you don't make a noise they won't take any notice."

COASTAL CLEANUP DAY in California, netted a stranger hoard of junk than organisers had ever imagined - it included a dead elk, a bottle of cockroaches and a laptop computer. Among other items found were televisions, a football helmet, 50,502 bits of foam, 48,743 bits of paper, 41,937 pieces of plastic, 41,937 food wrappers, 30,810 fragments of glass, 23,045 drinking straws and a dead dog with the leash still on.

A VANDAL in Darlington damaged seven Fiats - six Unos and one Tipo - in one night by forcing open the top of the doors and bending them outwards. Other makes of car were ignored.

A YELLOW D-registered Ford Sierra estate car ran into the back of a minibus on King's Avenue, Clapham, London on 26 January 1997. The minibus was driven by Ferrell Brown, 62, who was on his way back from a church service in Brixton with his wife and two other worshippers. According to Brown "The man got out of the car, opened the boot, took a bicycle out and rode off. A few minutes later he was back with a baseball bat. He started smashing his own car. He broke every single window, but never said a word. Then he jumped on the bike again and rode off. I was not shaken up by the accident - it was only a slight bump - but I was shaken up by what he did."

CHAPTER NINE

Pulling The Wool

Scams, hoaxes and pranks - just when you think you've seen them all someone comes up with a new twist.

IN BULGARIA school authorities were taking action to stop a thriving trade in fleas which had sprung up among schoolchildren. The insects were changing hands at the equivalent of 50p each because under education regulations pupils with flea infestations have to take 3 days off school.

PENSIONER Willy Klettner managed to blag more than 200 free rides from police and ambulance drivers in order to save money on taxi fares. Whenever he wanted to get home Willy, 71, would feign a heart attack - then claim the pills he needed to save him were at his house in Augsberg, Germany. They would rush him home where he would pretend to take his pills and recover. The police, however, tumbled his ruse and now have orders to take him directly to hospital if he tries it again.

IN BIHAR, India, a probe by the Accountant General's office revealed surprising feats achieved by the region's farmers. It seems they regularly transport bulls and buffaloes about the place on motor scooters. By transporting the creatures the farmers were eligible to claim various subsidies, but when some of the claims were examined in detail they found that scooter no BHV 9231 was used to transport bulls from Ranchi to Ghagra on 6 December 1985 and that numerous other small vehicles had been reported as achieving similar feat of cattle transportation in the subsidy claim documents.

A TRUCKER in Norway who reported his 60ft lorry stolen had his insurance scam rumbled when the "missing" vehicle was discovered buried in his garden.

COMEDIAN Franco Milano was determined to make sure his performance was a hit at his comedy club in Verona, Italy. He decided to leave nothing to chance, but was arrested by police after being caught pumping laughing gas round the audience during the show.

A HUNDRED phone subscribers in Lille, France, were cut off by a hoaxer who called them and said "Your line is interfering with police radio messages. Cut the cable immediately". They did. In Hamelin, Germany, a woman received a threatening phone call telling her "I've got your daughter. If you want to see her alive, burn your house down". It was only after she'd obeyed instructions that she discovered it was a hoax.

A WOMAN in Glendale, California, told police that she received a call from a man telling her he was conducting a survey for a shoe company. He asked her for her age, address, shoe size and favourite styles and brands. He promised her 40 pairs of shoes over the next year if she destroyed her old ones. The woman cut up a $70 pair while the man listened. When she called a number the man had given her, she reached the Hughes Aircraft Company. Hughes had received about 40 calls in the previous week from victims of the scheme, police said.

WHEN POLL TAX was introduced in the late 1980's authorities found themselves checking out a claims from the Queen of Sheba and the Venerable Bede in Stockton-on-Tees, and a whole assortment of other unlikely characters across the country. Council officers were forced to look into the names in case someone identifying with a historical or fictional character had actually changed their name by deed poll. Stockton's assistant treasurer Austin Cartwright said "A couple of people have not taken the form seriously, but we have to ask them if they have changed their names."

ROLF LESSINGER, barred from building a house on land he owned near Reisa in Germany, dug a huge crater, filled it with water and built a houseboat instead. The town has no planning laws for houseboats.

IN SWEDEN a man was refused a radio licence at half price after he claimed he should pay less on account of the fact that he was completely deaf in one ear.

IN LATE 1991 the normally reliable ticket machines on Stuttgart's urban railway system began to break down. On examination it was found that the innards of the machines were contaminated with liquid and the coin drums, which should have been full of DM5 coins were empty. The Germans put a team of private detectives on the case and they traced the problem to two children with water pistols which had been distributed as a free gift with a comic. When fooling around one had squirted water into the slot of a ticket machine with it, and to their surprise there was a clanking sound and the machine spat out a torrent of DM5 coins. Seeing a quick way to get rich they tried it on other machines, with the same result, but they couldn't keep the trick to themselves and soon all the city's children seemed to be doing it. By the time the authorities inserted plastic films and drains into the system to solve the problem, they had lost almost £750,000, but because most of the "criminals" were minors they couldn't recover the losses.

WHEN A VIEWER recorded an episode of the TV cartoon Rupert the Bear for his five-year-old grandson, he was shocked to see an array of pornographic magazines appear in one scene. The magazines Matrons in Leather, A Guide to Knickers and Spanking appeared only for a fraction of a second in the window of a shop Rupert is seen walking past, and had been missed by the TV station, the company who made the programme and thousands of other viewers. A spokesman said "It was somebody's idea of a joke, but we do not see the funny side. It was a totally irresponsible and unprofessional thing for one of the animators to do and we are going to find out who did it."

ART DEALER John Austin advertised in a Sydney, Australia, newspaper that he would supply "absolutely nothing" for $1; and 489 people replied enclosing cash.

CALVIN RUSSELL smuggled a sculpture into London's Tate gallery after successfully applying for permission to bring an easel in. Security men missed the 13in (33cm) tall brass-nickel sculpture and also failed to spot the plinth, which the young sculptor erected when their backs were turned. Shortly afterwards a friend brought in a display case and Iron Man was on display with a sign stating the work had been "donated" by the artist. Russell left the sculpture and went for a drink. When he returned, the gallery's security men were waiting for him, "They were very good. They said I could have the sculpture back, or they'd throw it in a skip." The sculpture was later on sale at the Rosemary Branch pub in Islington "It was £180" said Russell "but it's £350 now. After all, it has been on show in the Tate." In the 1970's Los Angeles artist Jeffrey Vallence was continually refused permission to show his work at the Los Angeles County Art Museum. Instead, he bought a number of electric wall sockets and painted them with "stupid little scientific scenes like microscopes and dinosaurs and cows and slabs of butter." Dressed as a janitor, he entered the museum and replaced the old sockets with his own, while friends kept a lookout for gallery guards. He wasn't caught. The sockets remained there for about two years until the galleries were repainted. Vallence believes the sockets are still there under several coats of paint and one day hopes to take them to an art restorer and have the paint removed.

BRUCE JENSEN of Bountiful, Utah, met a female doctor named Leasa Bibianna Herrera when working as a lab technician at University Hospital, Salt Lake City. She wore heavy make-up and a "Cleopatra Style" wig. She told Jensen that she was an Israeli disowned by her parents for marrying a non-Jew, and had later joined the Mormons. After a single sexual encounter, she told Jensen she was pregnant with twins and

Jensen felt morally obliged to give the children a father, so in December 1991 they were married. Several months later Herrera claimed to have cancer and said the twins were still-born. In April, however, she went to New York for cancer treatment and disappeared. Worried, Jensen filed a missing persons report on his wife, but was surprised at how police traced her. A man called Felix Urioste was pulled over for speeding in Nevada, and was found to have identification in 19 different names on him, including that of Leasa Bibianna Herrera. It seemed that Urioste had run away from home at 13 and told his family that he had had a sex change operation at 17, after which they referred to him as female. In fact he had never completed his gender reassignment and, while having had his testes removed, retained his penis. When he vanished in April he was wavering in his intention to complete the change and had stopped taking the hormones which gave him breasts - at the time of his arrest he had a thick moustache. He had managed to fool Jensen because he never allowed him to see him naked and the marriage was essentially celibate. On discovering his "wife's" true identity Jensen sought an annulment on the grounds of irreconcilable differences (not to mention unnatural similarities) and planned to return to his native Wyoming and "crawl into a hole for a few years".

ALSO somewhat surprised was Rosalinda de Hernandez. After her husband Gustavo was murdered, she was stunned to be told that he was, in fact, not only a woman, but pregnant too. Rosalinda, of Tegucigalpa, in Honduras, who had been married to Gustavo for nine years said: "Our love life was a bit strange, but I never suspected he was a woman."

A MUCH GREATER stir was caused by Edwin Baryion, 32, from the Philippines. He claimed to have been born a hermaphrodite and to have undergone surgery in 1985 to remove his penis and construct a vaginal passage. After taking hormones, he said, he began menstruating. After he missed a period in 1992 he went to see Dr Clarita Paggao, a gynaecologist in Malaybalay, who carried out tests and scans which revealed Edwin was six months pregnant. Along with his lover - a junior army officer named Roel Enriquez he announced to the world he was so happy he could cry. "Now I can prove to the world I'm a real woman," blubbed Edwin "I'm really feeling fulfilled." Hermaphrodites are usually sterile, so Edwin seemed a medical rarity of considerable interest, so much so that the Ministry of Health offered to pay all his medical expenses. His case created such a stir that a team of doctors from the World Health Organisation approached Edwin for an examination. They found him strutting around the hospital in a maternity gown, but he wouldn't allow them to examine him, so they rushed him and forced his pants down. What was revealed was an underdeveloped penis "the size of a thumb" and no sign of surgery or a vagina. The distended "pregnant" stomach was apparently the result of hormones, muscle control or gallons of Coca-cola. The doctor who had confirmed the pregnancy later admitted that Edwin worked in the hospital and, that as a co-worker, she'd trusted his word and hadn't actually examined him.

A FAITH HEALER was paid £50,000 by the Muret family of Thionville, France, to improve the exam performance of their 17-year-old son Francois, and told them that they had to drink a glass of ink and balance an egg on their heads to achieve this. They gave it a go - and Francois still finished bottom. The Murets sued the mystic.

CHAPTER NINE

INDONESIAN POLICE arrested a man in Jogjakarta for selling "magic pencils which, he claimed, would automatically produce correct answers in university exams. They confiscated about £2600 from the sales of the pencils, which had been on offer for almost a year. The man claimed the pencils were equipped with copper wire and produced electronic signals which would confuse the computers marking the exams and correct wrong answers. Dozens of students had complained when the magic did not work for them.

IN HEBEI province, China, Jing Taibao got himself into a lot of trouble over his patented "electronic height-raising devices". He had 27 factories apparently manufacturing the matchbox-sized device, which was then sold on to short adolescents in Beijing with the promise that it would make them grow 5-7 cm taller. It made Jing rich - until the complaints started to roll in. A TV actor claimed he applied the device to the designated acupuncture points on his body, but instead of becoming taller, his face grew ashen and pimply and his eyes swelled up horribly, ruining his career. His face recovered after 10 months, whereupon he found he'd actually become 1cm shorter. Another user complained the device caused two bloody holes in his leg, which went numb. Jing's patent was finally withdrawn after it was found he'd faked "clinical tests" by using a blank report sheet and stolen seal from a local hospital. However, not everything was disastrous for him - he still had a patent on a device for losing weight.

CHAPTER TEN

Lost Weekends

People have all kinds of reasons for hiding from the world - or hiding others from it.

A SAFFRON ROBED Buddhist climbed Cader Idris in north Wales in December 1996, so that he could commune with nature in peace during the winter solstice. Walkers saw him and reported encountering a lone climber with an apparent head injury, causing a team of 20 from the South Snowdon Mountain Rescue Volunteers to leave their Christmas party and head off up the 2,900ft mountain to rescue him, assisted by an RAF helicopter. They found the 50-year-old man, who came from Milton Keynes, sitting in a tent in sub-zero temperatures with a cut on his head caused by falling ice. He was not entirely pleased at having his meditations disturbed and, after assuring his would-be rescuers that he was fine and the cut was not serious, he asked them firmly, but politely to "go away".

CHAPTER TEN

A CHILD WELFARE worker visited Georgia Jackson's one-room Brooklyn apartment to investigate a report of child neglect. When she knocked at the door, Jackson, 39, opened the door brandishing a table leg and tried to drag the social worker into the apartment. She pulled herself free and fled, while neighbours called the cops. When they arrived they found Jackson's children - three boys aged 15, five and 10 months and a girl of three - confined to the flat and living in filthy conditions. The mother and three eldest children were dressed identically, wearing black smocks with white ceramic medallions around their necks. Police discovered that the three-year-old and the five-year-old had been shaved completely bald and had shoulder length blonde wigs glued to their heads. The three eldest children also wore nose rings and earrings. There was no fridge, no stove and only one mattress and all the children were malnourished. They were all "very quiet, very polite and very withdrawn." Jackson was arrested and the children taken into care.

IN LATE NOVEMBER 1991 an 11-year-old boy with an "angelic face and wild long blonde hair" was discovered by police hiding upstairs with his reclusive 31-year-old mother Rosemary in a semi-detached house in New Haw, Surrey. Behind windows obscured by bluebottles they lived in extreme squalor with 74 animals (a dog, cats, guinea-pigs, hamsters, rabbits, budgies, canaries and fish) 28 of them dead and many more dying with cages and hutches covered in excrement up to three inches deep. The corpse of one guineapig was mummified. Some of the rooms were piled so high with rubbish that it was impossible to walk on the floor. Hundreds of rats and mice scavenged on the debris. Food was kept in a 1940s Austin Eight in the garden, as the kitchen was crammed with rubbish. The boy hardly ever left the house, and then only in the company of his mother, and was forbidden to talk to anyone. Though he had never been to school his educational level was about normal for his age. medical reports suggested that neither the mother or son was suffering from any psychiatric illness. What was amazing was that, apart from birth registration, the child seemed to have eluded notice by all officialdom for his entire 11 years.

WHEN FIRE destroyed Ernest Dittermore's farmhouse, neighbours in Troy, Kansas, pooled their cash to buy the 60-year-old bachelor a trailer home. Grateful, Dittemore filled the trailer with food, then spent the night in a four-by-ten foot hole he'd dug in the ground with a shovel. 18 years later he was still living in his hole, using the trailer just for storage. "I'd been thinking about living underground for quite a while, even before the house burned", he said " It's a lot easier to heat. I can keep warm and save money on fuel costs". He sleeps on a bed of newspapers and uses a wood-burning stove for heat. A skylight built into a concrete slab covering the hole is blackened with smoke but still lets in a little light. There's no electricity or telephone. "Ernie is the nicest guy you'll ever meet said neighbour Jim Gilmore. "One day we'll find him dead in his hole; but he'll die happy."

ON 11 NOVEMBER 1977 police finally caught up with James Horton Jr when they trailed him to a 4-by 6 foot man-made cave in Santa Ana Canyon, California. For over a year this "phantom of the freeway" had been hurling rocks with great strength and accuracy at passing cars. At least 70 cars had shattered windscreens, dented hoods or damaged bodies. A deputy sheriff who gave chase was stabbed. The phantom eluded search parties by building camouflaged bridges across streams and setting false "camp-fires". He told his captors he lived this way because he "didn't want to be bothered by people".

CHAPTER TEN

IN FLANDERS, gravediggers at Ledeberg cemetery near Ghent opened a three-roomed family crypt in preparation for a burial and found a bed on a coffin, a gas cooker, sewing machine, electric razor, radio, dishwasher, coffee machine, books, records, rifle and rotting food. Electricity was provided by a stolen car battery placed outside the grave. Jules Roberts, a local tramp who had been in jail two years admitted creating the hideaway.

PC ROGER WARMAN was called to the flat of Miss Grace Slan, a retired dressmaker, in Scott Ellis Gardens, St. John's Wood, London, after neighbours complained of the smell. He found the 81-year-old recluse dead. Her one bedroom flat was lit with gas, a kettle hung over an open-range fire, there was art deco furniture and a newspaper with a headline on the General Strike of 1926. She had lived in the flat since 1914, initially with her father, and nothing at all had been changed since then. She wore old-fashioned clothes and shunned callers, not even letting the gas man in to read her meter. Her last known contact with the outside world was in 1959 when her father died and she was taken into hospital to get over it.

IN TILEHURST, Reading, Joan Abery, 70, was known to everyone by sight. She walked five miles to the library every day and would sometimes be seen running through the fields with her white hair flying behind her. Her face appeared to be painted with flour. After she was not seen for three weeks police visited her bungalow. They found Miss Abery's body in the garden inside a nest-like lean-to made of twigs and large umbrellas. The garden was piled with empty plastic boxes wrapped in pink ribbon, while the bungalow was completely enclosed in undergrowth and full of rubbish. Neighbours said Miss Abery, once a pharmacist, had refused to go back inside after being jilted at the altar 35 years before.

A SARDINIAN FARMER Antonio Angius, 57, kidnapped Pasquale Mereu, 47, and kept him captive for 15 years, working him as a sheepdog. He wore ragged canvas clothing, was fed on cheese and had to spend virtually 24 hours a day with 50 of the flock of 400 sheep. He was freed after villagers found him crawling on all fours, barking at sheep, and spent his first night in a bed for 15 years.

A GIRL locked in a dark room for more than six years because she had a headache was eventually freed by police. Carmela Borchetti was 16 when her uncle, a fortune teller, decreed that her headache meant she was possessed by evil spirits and the only cure was to spend seven years in a dark room. Carmela's parents put her in her bedroom and fastened the shutters. Her ordeal ended when someone tipped off social workers, who called at her home in Chieta, central Italy. Carmela, by now 22, pale, thin and hardly able to stand, at first insisted that she did not want to leave her prison. "Go away", she told police "I must lie here for six more months and then I can live again." Eventually, she was put on a special diet in Hospital. Her mother Maria, 49, and her father Francesco, a 62-year-old dustman, were not charged as, surprisingly, under Italian law, they had committed no offence.

ARNOLD DE LOUGHREY, 77, a weekend night-porter in Widnes, Cheshire, failed to turn up for work in January 1981. Firemen broke into his house and found him dead from a heart-attack. The house was full of evil-smelling garbage and in a nest of newspapers and rubbish which reached up to two feet from the kitchen ceiling they found his 77-year-old wife Edith wearing the tattered remains of a 1940's dress, and with long matted hair and 8 inch fingernails. She clawed and growled at her rescuers until given a sedative and taken to hospital.

Agoraphobia had kept her in the house for over 30 years. Mr De Loughrey's employer remarked "I couldn't understand how Arnold had always turned up for work smartly dressed until the police opened a garden shed. In it were found his suit and shirts which he used to wear to work."

THE APTLY NAMED News Horufu spent most of the 1970's chained naked to a tree 70 miles north of Harare, Zimbabwe, by his relatives because he was said to be possessed by evil spirits. In 1980 the demented man was freed and after treatment by Mrs Jelly Chari, one of the country's 30,000 traditional healers. In March 1981 a smiling News left her clinic and returned to his village. He said he was looking forward to returning to his parents and helping with the ploughing "There is no need to chain me anymore" he said. In Bellingham, north of Seattle, a five-year-old boy was tied to a chair for most of every day for a year by two women who described him as "cannibalistic". The boy's relationship to the women is not known.

FOR NEARLY eight years a Portuguese businessman, Antonio Verissimo, 65, kept his secret love affair from his fellow villagers in Alhos Vedros near Lisbon, by locking his mistress and their two daughters in a farm shed. Vivelinda Rodriguez was discovered and released in the summer of 1981 and was hospitalised for severe nervous disorders while her daughters, Ana, 7, and Rosa, 8, were cared for by nuns. The girls could not walk properly and knew only a handful of words. Verissimo was not arrested: police said they had no justification for detaining him. The boot was on the other foot for Mariano Jose da Silva, a Brazilian farmer. He was locked up in a windowless room and chained to the wall after catching his wife Antonia Maria in bed with her lover in 1983. For the next 13 years, Mr da Silva's wife fed him through a small hatch and threw the odd bucket of cold water over him so he could clean himself. Mr da Silva, 42, told the Correilo Braziliense newspaper: "At first I cried a lot, but then I got used to it." He was finally freed by cousins from Brasilia.

MIROSLAV KOLAK, a Yugoslavian religious fanatic, kept his eight children imprisoned from birth because the outside world was evil. When police raided his home in Melbourne, Australia they had to scale a 13 foot high wire fence and penetrate an elaborate security system including searchlights, sirens and electronic eyes. The eldest child, 21-year-old Alexander had somehow managed to escape with two brothers and a sister and had reported the situation to welfare authorities. Neighbours said they were unaware of the existence of the children.

FARIZBOURZ, 37, has incarcerated himself every day since 1980 to avoid conscription in Iran Every day his mother brings him newspapers so he can see if there's been an amnesty for draft-dodgers. Over the years of his self-incarceration his mental health has declined markedly. he is the youngest of six children. His mother said: "At the beginning we did not take it seriously, but gradually his seclusion rose to the point where he did not want to talk to anybody. His psychosis has reached the point where he hasn't visited the bathroom for four years, he just washes his hands with soap, although he always makes a fuss about my personal hygiene. He doesn't speak to his sisters and brothers and won't let me turn on the lamp in his room; when it gets dark he squats in the corner. he sometimes gets so nervous that he breaks all the dishes, and his room is full of old newspapers." His mother has not left the house herself for four years, fearing he may harm himself.

CHAPTER TEN

A THAI WOMAN was chained in a deserted hut for 13 years because her parents thought she was possessed by evil spirits. Chalauy Prathumasuth, 41, was freed from the hut in Uthong village of Suphan Buri province about 75 miles north of Bangkok and taken to hospital after police had been tipped off by a villager. Chalauy had begun acting strangely after her husband left her 13 years before, taking their baby son with him. Her illiterate parents decided that she was under the influence of a black magic spell cast by her husband and reasoned that the only way to protect her was to chain her up. At the time of the report police were investigating whether legal action could be taken against the parents.

CHAPTER ELEVEN

Off The Handle

It only takes a little thing to set some people off - but, boy, do they go for it!

A DISTRESSED GERMAN, seeking treatment for his frayed nerves, rammed his car into 41 other cars, parked it, then walked over another 19.

ARNALDO TIGALLI, a builder from Reggio, Italy, stabbed his friend Giuseppi Argussa in a bar, because he had refused to lend him his guitar - 31 years earlier. "He ruined my musical career" an indignant Arnaldo told police.

WAITRESS Hannah Finlander lost her job at a restaurant in Perth, Australia, after a customer sent back his stew demanding more meat in it, and she returned it with a dead mouse in the bowl. In La Paz, Bolivia, another waitress, Maria Vasquez, snapped after customer Luis Gomez complained that he has seen her sneeze in his soup as she served it and demanded she take it back. Vasquez refused, and forced Gomez to eat the soup at gunpoint.

A MAN with a complaint about child support walked into a social services office in Watkins Glen, New York, and shot four staff dead before committing suicide, while in Seoul, South Korea, another man killed five people with an axe when they tried to stop him committing suicide, before a relative shot him dead.

A SPANISH PRIEST drew a gun and opened fire on mourners who were complaining because he refused to accompany a coffin to the cemetery, injuring one man. He said the dead man did not attend mass often enough.

TO ENSURE he was declared winner at an amateur ballroom dance contest in Texas, Wayne Pearson held the judges at gunpoint. After police arrived and took him away, the judges reconsidered their verdict - and decided Pearson was still the winner.

MONIQUE BAZILE, a 57-year-old teacher at a high school in Irvington, New Jersey was arrested and faced eight years jail for endangering children's welfare and making threats after performing a voodoo ritual against a rowdy class of 13-year-olds. As the class ran riot she began shaking and chanting, threw powder on pupils, waved the cross at them and said their souls were going to the Lord. She also threatened to burn their houses down. In Xiantao, China, another teacher who had reached the limit was jailed for two years after forcing pupils to eat cow dung for not doing their homework.

WHEN Albert Simon's car broke down in the middle of New York frustration boiled over so he pulled out his gun and shot the Ford Mustang four times through the windscreen, startling his friend who was rummaging under the bonnet to find the fault. Simon, 28, ran away when he saw police approaching, but surrendered after a short chase. An officer said "I wouldn't want to be that guy's mechanic." A New Jersey man was mystified as to why police arrested him after he shot his computer - he failed to see why he couldn't shoot his own computer in the privacy of his own home. Police might have been more forgiving if he hadn't used illegal hollow-point bullets fired from an unregistered weapon.

IN KUWAIT a man was rushed to hospital with back pain and exhaustion after making love to his 17-year-old wife six times a day in the week after their wedding. "He was pale and powerless and could not speak" the Kuwaiti newspaper al-Watan reported. He had to be carried to the ambulance by friends because " he felt dizzy and had excruciating pain in his back, then collapsed in the living room".

ALSO OVERDOING it on the sex front was Indian Guru, Namdeo Dhaneshwar, 55, from Bombay. He chopped off his own penis after his wife complained that she could not cope with his constant lust. After she told him "No more sex for you, you're wearing me out" he fetched a knife, chopped off his tackle and bled to death.

WHEN a 26-year-old Kansas man looked in a mirror and thought he saw a satanic pentagram in the iris of his right eyeball he knew exactly what to do - he popped the eyeball out of his head, cut the connecting tendons with a knife, then flushed it down the toilet. In California, highly religious Creighton

Miller cut his left foot off because he believed he had sinned by treading on insects.

AFTER HIS pet mongrel dog, Lucky, was run over and killed, Stuart Fergusson from Strathbungo, Glasgow, was so distraught he hacked off his own hand. He took a chisel to his right wrist, finished the job with a hacksaw, then asked a neighbour to call an ambulance. However, while doctors were preparing to reattach the hand, Stuart, 42, vanished, sparking off a massive three hour search of the city's southside using helicopters. Eventually he was found hiding in a workman's hut in Pollock park, having walked two miles and swum the White Cart river. He was returned to the Victoria Infirmary where doctors tried to reattach the hand again.

A TELEPHONED bomb threat that forced a Jordanian airliner to land in Iceland was caused by a woman trying to prevent her mother-in-law accompanying her to Chicago. The plane was en-route from Amsterdam to Chicago when a caller contacted Royal Jordanian Airlines and named a woman on board who she said had a bomb. The culprit turned out to be a newly wed woman who was travelling to Chicago with her husband for their honeymoon - accompanied by his mother.

ALSO CAUSING airline trouble was Kostas Tsenkides, who was arrested for attempting to hijack an Olympic Airlines jet. Tsenkides, 24, was released on bail when he explained that he was in a panic after swallowing a crucifix on take-off. When the pilot refused to believe it had lodged in his throat, the choking youth threatened to blow up the plane unless it made an emergency landing.

AFTER his father explained that the tooth fairy would pay him £2 for every tooth found under his pillow, seven-year-old Jonathan Reohorn decided to leave nothing to chance. Instead of letting things proceed naturally, he crept downstairs and borrowed a pair of pliers from his father's toolbox which he used to pull five of his teeth out in a bid to cash in. Jonathan, from Pendine, Dyfed, Wales, claimed that the teeth pulling did not hurt and only took a few minutes.

A MOROCCAN was arrested in northern Spain after he dumped his wife and one of his five children beside a motorway because, he said, his car was overloaded. The family was returning to Belgium after holidaying in Morocco and had 800 miles to go.

GRETA HAGEL from Stuttgart, out shopping, was splashed by a motorist as he drove through a puddle. She noted the number plate, tracked him down a few days later and shot him dead. When Michael Debaets, 49, came home to Santa Clara, California, from holiday with his family, he found, his newspaper soaked with what he believed to be dog urine from the dog belonging to his neighbour, Martin Myslinski, 33. An argument ensued between Debaets' wife and Myslinski, during which Debaets, without saying a word, shot his neighbour in the chest. Myslinski died in hospital an hour later.

JOSEPH FALLAR Sr, 61, was arrested at his house in Harrison City, Pennsylvania, for the murder of his wife, Florene, 50, whom he had stabbed 219 times. "He told me he killed his wife" said patrolman John Simcoviak. " He said she would stack the refrigerator full of vegetables, hiding the milk, and he wasn't going to take that anymore."

TRIVIAL arguments can easily get out of hand. Michael Wrightman, 30, pleaded guilty in Toronto in February 1993 to beating David Marlatt to death over which of them had the longer criminal record. The following month, a man shot dead his best friend during an argument over whether a woman was wearing knickers in a bar in Benton, Illinois. That November, Edward Hammond, 27, was shot dead in Baton Rouge, Louisiana, during an argument over the proper way to season a roast turkey.

IN A BANGKOK karaoke bar, Thai property tycoon Chen Ka Sek hogged the microphone for three hours and sang Candle in the Wind four times. When another man asked to have a go, Mr Sek had his bodyguards shoot the presumptuous individual dead. "We were carried away by the beauty of my voice," Mr Sek confessed.

FOR SIX years Linda Rosenberg had lived in apparent harmony next to Eleanor and Alan Brewer and their four children in Melbury Gardens, Wimbledon. One evening in June 1993, when the Brewers were relaxing at home with friends, Rosenberg poured 77 pounds of rotting chicken entrails, maggots and cockroaches down their chimney. It landed with a thud at the back of the gas fire. "It was revolting," said Mrs Brewer. "I've never smelt a dead body, but that's what I imagine one would smell like." Later Rosenberg appeared at their door with a replica gun and threatened to shoot Mr Brewer and his children. During Rosenberg's trial, she said she'd done it because she believed the Brewers had taken her puppy.

AUCTIONEER Des Lismore, 52, awoke on his sofa in Fillongley, Warwickshire, to see a clip on the TV from the film Independence Day in which Sky newsreader Bill Friendly warned that gigantic spaceships were heading for Earth. Lismore roused his young sons and ordered them to take blankets, food and water to the cellar. He sprinted to Fillongley Working Men's Club, burst in and shouted: "There's going to be an almighty bang!" He told the barmaid one spaceship was heading for America and she exclaimed "My God, my son's in Mexico!"

BRIAN YINGER, 42, a policeman in Dearborn, Michigan, was suspended in November 1992 and sent to a psychiatrist because he writes the number 7 in the European style, with a horizontal line through the downstroke. Six months earlier he had been instructed to break the habit he had acquired when he was 12 because "the way he was writing was confusing the typist". However, he forgot while writing some reports and as a result was suspended for three days without pay.

HAPPY STEWART, 16, appeared at Falkirk Sheriff Court and admitted assaulting a man, hitting a table with a broom handle and breaking crockery. She said she was "fed up" with being called Happy, a name that didn't suit her, and decided to change it to Elizabeth. She agreed to undergo anger management counselling and was fined £30.

AFTER being questioned by the FBI, Daniel Rudolph of South Carolina cut off his left hand with a circular saw, filmed the amputation and sent the video to the FBI as a protest. They were searching the mountains of North Carolina for his brother Eric Robert Rudolph, a suspect in the bombing of an abortion clinic in Birmingham, Alabama. Surgeons struggled to reattach the hand.

CHAPTER ELEVEN

A 41-YEAR-OLD shopper in Milwaukee cut off part of Vickie Lemon's nose with a pocket knife in the parking lot of Kohl's Food Store because the latter had gone through the "10 items or less" express checkout with too many items in her trolley.

CHAPTER TWELVE

A Man's Gotta Do What A Mans Gotta Do

The sheer range and variety of human compulsions and obsessions is simply beyond belief

POLICE in New Jersey spent some time pursuing a thief with a strange fetish. He held nine people at gunpoint over a one-month period - and demanded they hand over their garden spades. "This is one big weirdo on the loose" said a police officer.

MARIETTE THOMAS, 39, got a divorçe from husband Claude, 41, because he was obsessed with throwing eggs. In court in Bordeaux, France she complained "It was funny when it started a few years ago but now its out of control." On the other hand an Israeli woman divorced her husband because he was obsessed with Hillary Clinton. "When my husband heard that the Clintons were coming to Israel, he lost all control," the unnamed woman explained. "He waited in front of their Jerusalem hotel for hours just to see his beloved...a month ago, my husband surprised me by ordering me to colour my hair to match the shade used by the president's wife and to copy her hairstyle" Mrs Clinton's spokesman, Neel Lattimore said "It sounds to me like he's the one who needs the total make-over.

JOSE MOURA has made a career for himself as a "serial kisser". Known for kissing athletes, politicians and visiting dignitaries in Rio de Janeiro, he was hurled off a tennis court while trying to kiss Martina Navratilova as she played a match against Monica Seles. He had better luck with the Pope, succeeding in kissing John Paul II's feet during a papal visit in 1980.

LESS KIND to priests was Ettore Gaggliano, 86, who ended up in a psychiatric hospital after punching a cleric in the Milan Duomo - his 158th holy victim. A great grandfather whose offspring adore him and take pride in his reputation, Ettore said "I'm quite sane. I have a mission in life. Previously, having punched out a Greek Orthodox priest after ambushing him from behind a pillar, he explained proudly "there is nothing you can do to save the priests from me. I shall bash them all until my last breath." Normally acquitted in court due to his advanced years, he averaged one priest-bashing a month.

REYKJAVIK ZOO KEEPER Kennet Alboury ran into trouble when he encountered Brunella the penguin. A colleague explained "He never left her enclosure. He wouldn't look after any other animals. He just said 'Brunella needs me' " He was fired after he was found dressing the penguin in female underwear, despite his protestations that it was only to keep her warm. A zoo official said "How he was supposed to do this with a sexy bra and suspenders is anybody's guess." Kennet in the meantime began a new career as a taxidermist's assistant. Reflecting on his zoo experience he commented sadly "For a while my life was perfect. But now she's gone and I'm stuffing squirrels."

MADRID POLICEMAN Jose Aubrizo was fired on the spot when his bosses discovered his cache of 1,000 stolen teddy bears hidden in his house. He was sent to a psychiatrist to have his cuddly toy addiction treated.

DOCTORS were deeply confused when presented with four-year-old Stuart Elton's unusual phobia - he is completely terrified of poppers, buttons and toggles. Every time his mother, Elaine Elton, 28, tries to dress him in clothes fastened by any of these, he screams the house down. Instead Stuart has to be clothed in items fastened with elastic, velcro or zips. "Nobody knows why he has this phobia. He's seeing a psychologist every week." said his exasperated mother, desperately trying to assemble a buttonless uniform for the boy's first day at school. Dr Peter Hayward, of the Institute of Psychiatry, said "A lot of children have fears - like dogs or the dark - but this is very unusual."

LILY MEEHAM'S fear is hardly less peculiar - she has a mortal terror of bagpipes. She shakes uncontrollably, breaks into a sweat and her legs turn to jelly at even the faintest strain of Scottish music. Retired postal worker, Lily, 60, turned to psychiatry to cure her bizarre fear after she had to turn down an invitation to Scotland in case she heard pipes. Lily, of Anfield, Liverpool said "If I hear Mull of Kintyre I go to pieces", which is entirely understandable, and probably not reliant on bagpipe phobia, "New Year's Eve is a nightmare. I switch off the TV in case I hear a piper. I'm petrified of the noise - I've no idea why."

ROBERT DORRICOTT'S OBSESSION also had doctors thoroughly puzzled, they could find no explanation for his compulsive bicycle thefts. He once cycled 160 miles to London from his Rotherham home on a stolen bike - then gave it to a guard to pay for his train fare home. Perhaps he should have teamed up with the mysterious Chester litter bug who vexed the city's environmental officers by speeding through the city at midnight on a bike, strewing meticulously cut blank two-inch squares of paper in his wake. Council officials set up a telephone hotline for sightings in an attempt to catch the man.

BURGLAR Arnold Collins, 20, added an extra twist to his crimes. When caught after more than 30 offences, he confessed to surprised cops that he couldn't resist tickling his victim's feet as they slept. In Bonn, Germany, police were hunting someone who went a stage further. There someone was breaking into women's homes, drugging them - then giving them an expert manicure. Leeds University officials had a slightly different problem - the Marshmallow Man. He stared at female students before dropping a marshmallow and a note at their feet. Security staff captured the individual - described as having a pudding-bowl haircut - on one occasion, but he managed to make a break for it and escaped again.

ON THE University of Virginia campus at Charlottesville, someone was preying on women, rugby tackling them and making off with their clogs, while in Mexborough, Yorkshire, a "young man" waylaid a 10-year-old girl and robbed her of a single shoe. In Hilleroed, Denmark, a 70-year-old man was jailed for stealing 5,000 shoes over a seven year period. He refused to give a motive.

TOKYO POLICE arrested a cartoonist on suspicion of making 24,000 prank phone calls over a three-year period to a magazine that had refused to publish his work. Other cases in Japan included a woman of 55 who phoned a former teacher 28,000 times in a year to complain about alleged mistreatment when she was at school, and a 42-year-old man who had called his ex-wife 113,000 times over a 17-month period.

IN EUREKA, California, police were hunting a woman who had been grabbing babies from total strangers and breast-feeding them. "Every child needs lactate nourishment," she told a shocked mother during one incident.

NEIL GORDON WILSON suffered ill health all his life, and preferred to live an isolated life away from most of humanity. He didn't reckon much to humans - his greatest obsession was to be a fish. When he was found dead on 29 November 1995, in a field near Lake Toolondo in Victoria, Australia, he was clad from head to foot in a fish suit. Made from heavy green plastic salvaged from discarded water beds, the suit had round holes for eyes, but no holes for the nose or mouth or any other kind of ventilation - how he managed to breathe in there is something of a mystery. It covered both hands and feet. Both legs fitted into one 'leg' and the suit zipped up at the back with a single large zipper. The tight fitting garment severely restricted movement: his trunk and legs could only have moved back and forward in a dolphin-like manner. However, the suit's careful construction did leave the arms free to move up and down like fins. Encased in this suit, or another orange version found in his garage, Wilson would spend the majority of his time floating in Toolondo Lake, supported only by a rope from an overhanging tree as he swung and swum in the cool waters. Strangely, when he was found, his suit-clad corpse was a kilometre from the lake, which even at the fastest speed he could be expected to manage in the costume, would have taken him 14 hours to traverse. There were no vehicle tracks nearby, no signs of other human activity, and no track such as would have been left if he'd wiggled the distance. The week his body had lain in the field left it too decayed to establish a cause of death, and police concluded it was probably a bizarre form of suicide, although they hadn't ruled out foul play. They were doing their best to ignore the strange hint of teleportation.

ANIMAL OBSESSIONS take a variety of forms, with some individuals getting overwhelmed by the sheer number they accumulate. Environmental health officers found more than 200 animals in Michelle Parrish's house in Tonypandy, Wales. They included eight goats, three sheep, two Shetland ponies, 12 chickens, 12 ducks, five geese, four turkeys, two owls, two mynah birds, a parrot, a kestrel, assorted pigeons, cockateels, doves, quail and budgies....plus ten rabbits, three hamsters, six ferrets, seven rats, three tortoises, a python, a guinea fowl, other reptiles, amphibians and fish, a Vietnamese pot-bellied pig, 22 dogs and countless cats. Taken to court, she was allowed to keep 12 rodents in a shed, two snakes, plus birds and the pot bellied pig. After the hearing she said "this will make everything a lot easier."

IT'S NOT just cat remains that get hoarded either, Lai Siang Kwong from Singapore got fined £5,000 for keeping the cremated remains of 2,000 people in his bungalow. It was the fourth time he had been convicted of using his bungalow to house funeral urns.

CHAPTER THIRTEEN

Who Told You You Were Naked?

Adam and Eve may have been embarrassed to find they were naked, but this lot certainly weren't!

FISH HATCHERY MANAGER Bill Bowling knew something was amiss when he spotted a naked man near one of his ponds in San Marcos, Texas. When he asked him what he was doing the man explained he was Jesus and had just fallen to Earth. Not entirely believing him, but suspecting this had something to do with a solar eclipse the previous day, Bowling asked the intruder to leave, which he tried to do by walking across a hatchery pond. He fell in up to his neck and refused to come out. Bowling called the police, who arrived in considerable numbers. Faced with a Jesus impersonator neck deep in a hatchery pond, and by now ranting in an unknown language, they were temporarily phased, as none were eager to go in after him and they felt it unwise to use electric stun guns on someone who was mostly underwater, so Bowling agreed to drain the pond. He was saved the trouble when another cop arrived and recognised "Jesus" as a local mentally ill man. Calling him by name, he told him to get out the pond or face the consequences, upon which "Jesus" said "Oh, OK", calmly climbed out and was taken to the local psychiatric hospital. The following day a female visitor to the hatchery had a six-foot-long boa constrictor fall out from under her car when she stopped - the woman had no idea where it came from.

THE BOOT was on the other foot in Hunter Mountain, New York State, there it was the police who were naked. New York City cop Peter Panariello ended up under arrest after he was struck by a car while running naked through the ski resort with a woman he had kidnapped draped over his shoulder. "I was walking with a friend...when a man I did not know ran over to us" Diane Melia said, "when he couldn't get a grip on my friend he threw me over his shoulder...he ran into traffic and we were hit". Panariello, who was staying in the town with other officers from the Coney Island Avenue station was not drunk, but gave no reason for his behaviour.

MORE ROMANTIC was the encounter between Edna Ourbach and Daniel Tevereau. Australian teacher Ourbach was eating at a cafe in Majorca when the naked Tevereau crashed onto her table from above. He had woken up in his hotel room overlooking the cafe and had toppled over his balcony while looking for the toilet. Neither person was injured in the surprise encounter. They married three weeks later.

JOGGERS seem partial to doing it in the buff, but always with a strange twist. Police in Nottinghamshire spent sometime hunting a jogger who was sighted in the county accompanied by a dog. The man was naked, but the dog was wearing a plastic coat. Just up the road in Heanor, Derbyshire, another nude jogger was seen on several occasions running through Shipley Park. Slim, and aged about 40, he always carried a pair of purple underpants. These two seem to have evaded identification, not so keep-fit fanatic Dr Keith Rose, 31. He was forced to resign after being seen out jogging in Georgia, USA - naked, but with an empty paint tin on his manhood.

ALSO going for strange embellishment was a flasher who, since April 1992 has exposed himself to over 50 women in Australia - he has a padlock clamped round his genitals. Another flasher, this time in Lyons, France ended up with a strangely embellished penis, although he had not intended to. After exposing himself repeatedly, 40-year-old Maurice La Salle was accosted by a gang of vengeful women who pinned him down and super-glued a Donald Duck hand-puppet to his penis. They then tore off his clothes and left him to go to hospital "wearing nothing but the duck" according to police. Far luckier was Spencer R Schosnagle, who, has been repeatedly voted in as Mayor of Friendsville, Maryland, despite numerous convictions for exposing himself, some while he was actually in office. One of his supporters said "If we look in our own closets, I'm sure there would be skeletons".

A WOLVERHAMPTON woman had an unexpected encounter with a Lone Ranger fan early one morning in 1990. She observed 55-year-old Derek Gill walking through the city wearing a coat draped over his shoulders, a Lone Ranger mask - and nothing else. Writing on the mask drew attention to what he described as "his naked Tonto" and a blue cord running from his neck to the organ he was describing animated it dramatically when he nodded his head. After he was arrested and charged with indecent exposure, Gill's lawyer explained he walked around like this "to relieve an irritating skin condition", although police later revealed the unlikely information that he had been banned from several nudist clubs "because of his unusual dress sense".

FILMS also seem to have had an influence on a naked man in Nashville, Tennessee. He gatecrashed a vegetable show, grabbed a champion carrot and scoffed it while screaming "What's up, doc?" like Bugs Bunny.

IN CORSICA Sean O'Mally, 27, from Waterford, Ireland hit serious trouble when he tried to flout a nudity ban on local beaches. He was pounced on by two burly locals who painted him bright red from head to toe. Also offended by nudity is one resident of Margate, Kent - they keep covering the top half of a naked Greek sea goddess statue in the shopping centre with woolly jumpers.

TWO DISTRACTED drivers crashed in Los Angeles when they saw a nude woman walking along the road. Paramedics called to the accident found Valerie Morales, 27, lying naked in the street, so they put her in the ambulance and went to check on the men, neither of whom were seriously hurt. As they did so, Morales leapt off the stretcher and drove off in the ambulance, causing mayhem as she headed north on the southbound lanes of the Glendale Freeway until she collided with a bread van and was arrested. In Columbia, South Carolina, Melvin Johnson, 29,a resident of the Salvation Army hostel for the homeless piled up his clothes and set them on fire, causing the building to be evacuated and the firebrigade to be called. Once they arrived, the naked man jumped into the fire chief's car and hurtled off across the city with all its lights blazing, with police in hot pursuit.

POLICE in Vinton, Louisiana, stopped a 1990 Pontiac Grand Am on 19 August 1993 after reports that it contained naked people. The driver got out wearing only a towel, but then jumped back in and crashed into a tree. Officers looked on slack-jawed as 20 completely naked people ranging in age from one to 65 and including three pregnant women and five children , piled out of the wreck and began religious chants. The car was a write off, but the injuries were all minor because the vehicle was so tightly packed. The party were all Pentecostals from Floydada, a small Texas town on their way to a religious retreat in Florida. Driver Sammy Rodriguez, 29, and his brother Danny said they were preachers. The Floydada police had been hunting for them for two days since relatives reported them missing. The Rodriguez brothers had declared that the devil was after them and that Floydada would be destroyed if they stayed there. The group, who were all related, left Floydada in five or six cars, abandoning them and their belongings along the way. They stripped because their clothes were possessed by the devil.

IN JANUARY 1997, a policeman had his attention drawn to three adults and two children, all naked, dancing round a car parked on the Western Freeway at Melton near Melbourne, Australia. As he approached the car , they jumped into the vehicle and drove off. Minutes later, the car stopped and a naked man got out to speak to the police. Two women and the children - boys aged 22 months and three years - took off and were chased at speeds of up to 87 mph (140km/h). At

Gordon, the car slowed down and one of the women holding the younger boy was forced out. The driver took off at speed again before finally being intercepted at Ballarat after driving over a roundabout. The 27-year-old woman driver told Ballarat Magistrates court the next day that she was attempting to exorcise demons from her two sons. She was driving naked into a red sunrise to cleanse the souls of the people in the car. She thought the police were demons coming to get her.

BOTH DRIVERS in a two-car crash in Ronda, Spain, were completely naked when cut from their vehicles. "One guy said the collision stripped him. But we don't believe him." said a police spokesman.

POLICE INVESTIGATED claims that smartly-dressed men were stripping off their suits and dancing naked in woodland near Penn Common, Sedgely, on the edge of the Black Country. Local residents had expressed worries about their children who play in the same area. "We just do not know what these men are up to," said Supt Malcolm Gough. "We do not know whether they are genuine nudists, nature lovers, or if they have more sinister motives...we have not caught anybody yet. Several local people claim to have seen them. "It's been going on, on and off, for about a year, although it seems to stop after November," said resident Judy Bardburn, She added "People who have seen them say all that they wear are black shoes and black socks."

IN BIASSA, Italy, a naked man was arrested after dancing daily at noon in a cemetery. The unemployed farmhand, who had to be protected from furious widows by police, said "It was the only pleasure I had in life."

STAFF at the Pot and Plant centre in Kidnappers Lane, Leckhampton near Cheltenham, were puzzled by what they found on 27 January 1996. Shoe prints led from the nursery to a pile of clothes (hooded jacket, size nine men's boots, socks and a PVC flat cap). Beyond the clothing a set of bare footprints led to a hawthorn bush. Police were stumped.

A TRAIN CREW made an emergency stop at Darien, Connecticut, at 2.30 am as they thought they had run over a body. When they shone their torches onto the track, a naked man, lying in the space between the rails, jumped up and attacked the three crew members before fleeing into nearby woods. One conductor was bitten twice in the leg and cut on his face while a second had a finger bitten. Artay Drinks, 23, of Bridgeport was arrested about an hour later and booked on assault and trespassing charges.

A CONVENIENCE STORE clerk was so stunned to see a completely naked man walk into the Big Apple store in Portland, Maine at 4am during a snowstorm that he didn't notice the 3ft (1m) sword that he was carrying. Michael Hicks, 29, came into the store and walked to a beer cooler without saying a word. The clerk asked Hicks to leave, whereupon he raised the double-edged sword and pointed it at the clerk's chest, saying "I'm thirsty". The clerk raised his hands and backed away. As he called the police, Hicks left the store without taking anything. He walked a few blocks before being spotted by police. he was arrested without a struggle. Police told him to keep away from the Big Apple store, whether he had clothes on or not.

A TEENAGE GIRL amazed customers at McDonald's in Croydon by ordering a burger then stripping off before eating it - they applauded. Two teenagers outside Tasty Pizza in Columbia Heights, Minnesota got a lower key reception. Late one night they turned their backs to the front window, dropped their pants and mooned at patrons, who ignored them. Upset that they were not being noticed they began to jump up and down. One of the two lost his balance, fell into the window, breaking it and cutting his buttocks and several fingers.

ALSO on the pizza front a man claiming to be a pizza delivery man, but wearing nothing but a baseball cap, went door-to-door in an apartment building. He was arrested only after injuring himself in the groin while trying to escape sheriff's deputies. Police were certain he was not a pizza delivery man, but remained unsure whether he was actually carrying a pizza. "Spring always brings this stuff out" said police dispatch supervisor Linda Wyland, "You always get these guys trying to show off what they have." This was also the excuse police gave for a man who interrupted traffic by running naked across the M5 near Gloucester, they reckoned he was celebrating the first day of spring.

A FAT STRIPPOGRAM man turned out to be nothing of the sort. The balding 40-year-old stripped off at an office in Ulm, Germany. Then police found the agency he claimed to be from did not exist. Also trying it on was "Sexy Marianne" who lured men round to her home with an ad in a contact magazine promising "Air Hostess, 34, lonely, long legs, hungry for love". When randy men arrived on her doorstep she shouted at them through the letter box, telling them to strip so she could see if she liked their body. Then Marianne dashed out shrieking that she was the victim of a flasher and demanding £60 hush money - she was not the sexy nymphomaniac they had been expecting, but a pensioner of 75. Over one hundred men who replied to her ads were conned, they said she had a voice far younger than her years, but she was exposed when one man went to the police.

AN INQUIRY into a Canadian phone company was launched after operators played a hoax on a complaining client. Harry Bole was told to strip naked "because of static" and jump "to test reception". Meanwhile, in Lancashire, police were looking for "The Catalogue Man" who had toured housing estates for four years persuading wives to strip off for "mail-order book model tests" - he had conned more than 40 victims into undressing.

JOSEPH LEE DAVIDSON, 22, apparently exhausted after a night of running naked through the streets of Hemet, California, broke into a house to take a nap. The homeowner found his front window broken apparently with a bicycle that had been taken from the garage, and Davidson in his bedroom, sleeping soundly under blankets. The police had earlier received several calls about a naked man running through parking lots.

A POLICEMAN in Ogden, Utah, spotted a small car parked in a cul-de-sac in the Ogden City Cemetery, rocking on its wheels. Inside was a partially clothed man banging his head violently against the steering wheel and "doing unnatural things with several squash-like vegetables." He was cited for lewdness, but insisted he had done nothing wrong.

QUEBEC provincial police were hunting for a man who took his clothes off, put a bag over his head and ran through the woods near Trois-Rivieres on several occasions over a three-week period. Police spotted him once and gave chase, but he escaped by jumping over a flooded ditch which the pursuing officers couldn't manage to cross.

IN SAN ANTONIO, Texas a man pulled off his clothes and started quacking like a duck when his bank denied him a loan. Police called to Bank One found the 40-year-old man naked in the vice-president's office. When questioned he only responded with quacks so the police took him in for psychiatric observation.

CHAPTER FOURTEEN

Everyone's Doing It!

People like to join in - however daft things may seem

STARTING in Sheffield, the craze for "tumbling" gripped teenagers during 1995. Described by medical authorities as "a very risky activity which shouldn't be encouraged", tumbling is simple in concept, if baffling in motivation. It simply involved climbing into the dryers of the local laundrette, having a friend close the door, put money in the slot and set the machine going. After a lengthy spin the tumbler emerged feeling dizzy and with a bloody nose. A spokesman for Pepe Jeans, who were forced to withdraw a series of commercials capitalising on the craze explained "It may sound bizarre, but this is what kids do - teenage life is pretty edgy."

CHAPTER FOURTEEN

THE YEAR before, Israel had been in the grip of an even odder mass obsession - cat-tossing. This involved hurling unwanted household pets out of cars on busy highways, intended to prevent them finding their way home, even if they survived the tossing. Most popular site for the "sport" was the eight-lane coastal highway heading north from Tel Aviv, from where almost 50 reports of tossing incidents were received by Lev L'chai, the Israeli animal protection organisation, who campaigned vigorously against the activity. Several road accidents had been caused by cat-tossers on the highway.

PRESUMABLY a southern Californian trend might have helped. Since 1995, baptising cars has been taking off there in a big way. Owners believe they can prevent them having accidents by mumbling incantations while sprinkling vodka over them.

IN EGYPT panic broke out after a rumour spread claiming that women were being driven to sexual frenzy after chewing gum laced with aphrodisiacs peddled by agents of Israel. Despite laboratory analysis finding nothing in the gum which could cause sexual arousal, sermons were preached against the brands and authorities in some areas banned suspect gum. Several young women confessed to being victims of the sex gum attack, one, named only as Amira, said "I lived the experience deeply and truly" explaining that she had accepted a lift and then some gum from two male classmates after which she began to lose control. "At the beginning, I thought that this feeling was just because I was alone with them in the car," the woman said, "But gradually I was beginning to wish that one of them was with me in the back seat. I was so easy. I found no resistance. And you know the rest." Sayada Abdul Moniem, a 20-year-old highschool graduate said "Women should be more prudent. I now chew a brand of gum that is made in Egypt. It is not very good quality, but at least it is safe."

WORSE STILL were the assaults on their sexual integrity men in Cameroon believed they were experiencing. They hanged at least three men accused of using evil powers to cause male genitals to disappear merely by shaking hands. Most of the alleged snatchers were Nigerian. An 18-year-old student said that, when he shook hands with a Nigerian friend, "he felt an electric-like current run through him, and a feeling that his manhood had retreated into his stomach." Doctors said all the "missing" tackle were unharmed and normal. In Malaysia, the population has periodically gone through similar panics, experiencing an affliction known as "Koro", or "Shook Yang". In these cases sufferers were seized by a delusion that their penis was retracting into their body, leading to imminent death, accompanied by intense panic, feelings of collapse, nausea, breathlessness, blurred vision, bodily spasms and pain. Sufferers tried to avert terminal dick retraction in various painful and imaginative ways, gripping the retreating member with chopsticks, tying it to a bedpost with string, safety pinning it to a leg or clamping it with a small jeweller's weighing instrument called a lie teng hok. Among suggested cures was the ingestion of powdered ashes from burned female undergarments. In every case examined by doctors the genitals were intact, in place and the only injuries they suffered were from the extreme methods used to prevent the imagined retractions.

IN GUATEMALA it was more vital organs which were rumoured to be vanishing - livers hearts and lungs. A number of American tourists were lucky to escape with their lives after mobs set upon them, accusing them of trying to steal children so that their organs could be sold for transplant in the US. After a particularly lurid rumour circulated in Santa Lucia, alleging that the corpse of an eviscerated child had been found flung in a ditch with a handful of dollars stuffed into its abdomen along with a note reading "Thank you for your collaboration" backpacker Melissa Larson was taken into police custody for her own protection when locals decided she was involved. After she was moved to another town for greater safety Santa Lucians overwhelmed a 500-strong riot squad, sacked the police station and burned it along with 10 vehicles. It took the army to restore order, injuring 50 people in the process.

IN 1989 an appeal was put out on behalf of 10-year-old Craig Shergold, then a patient in the Royal Marsden Hospital suffering from cancer. It asked people to send him get well cards to build his morale by providing him with the goal of getting into the Guinness Book of Records as the person to receive the greatest number of get well cards ever. This got massive publicity in the press and soon the Royal Marsden was so overwhelmed it had to ask people to send the cards to Craig Shergold's home address, although Guinness soon popped up and explained there was no such record in their book. This did not deter people, by October 1990 he had received 16,250,692 cards, with no sign of the flood stopping, the appeal being spread through the nascent internet worldwide. Since then, Craig has completely recovered and is now nearly 20, but the internet still regularly spreads appeals for get well cards on behalf of his 10-year-old self, or some variation on the theme. Some ask for business cards, others for bottle caps, crisp packets or old stamps to be sent to various hapless manufacturers so a sick child can get a wheelchair/iron lung/trip to Disneyland. All totally untrue, Craig, though, has become immortalised in net lore - such rumours are known as "Shergolds".

AFTER WEEKS of a Pepsi promotion intended to topple Coca Cola in one of the world's biggest soft drink markets, the Philippines, in summer 1992 Manila TV news announced that anyone holding a Pepsi bottle cap marked 349 would win up to a million pesos (about £27,000) tax free. The number 349 should have been accompanied by a seven digit security number - but wasn't, due apparently to a computer error. Up to 800,000 bottle caps marked 349 were in circulation, and by September 1993, 486,170 cap-holders had claimed billions of pounds - but Pepsico refused to pay. More than 10,000 criminal cases were filed against the company by angry consumers. Mobs of vengeful "winners" took to stalking the streets, so that Pepsi executives had to hire bodyguards and vary their routes to elude them. Guards rode shotgun on Pepsi trucks, which were stoned, torched or overturned, or, in one case, blasted with a fragmentation grenade. When one was firebombed in central Manila, the crew had to use the cargo to put the fire out. Protest rallies were held regularly, at one a woman proclaimed "Even if I die here, my ghost will come back to fight Pepsi!"

ALSO IN THE PHILIPPINES a cult called The Reserved Manpower of the Good Wisdom For All Nations distributed a leaflet which proclaimed that deflating tyres was "God's way of stopping bad deeds". Members of the cult then hired several jeeps, which carry about 15 people each and fanned out across Manila during evening rush hour. At their destinations they ordered the drivers out, let out the air from the jeep's tyres and then ran about deflating tyres on hundreds of other cars, buses and trucks, paralysing traffic throughout the city for several hours. Terrified motorists ran for cover as armed police pursued the pack of tyre deflaters who swarmed through stalled traffic deflating more tyres while waving streamers and placards bearing religious messages. When pressed for an explanation Reserved Manpower asserted "This is God's order to let out air - air is from God. This is the solution to the crisis in our country."

IN NORTHERN INDIA a strange outbreak occurred in 1991. Psychologists were sent to Garo Para village by the Tripura State Health Services to investigate reports that people in the village had been behaving abnormally for several days. They would sing, dance and cry until exhausted as though affected by mass hysteria. Others fled the village in panic.

UNUSUAL industrial unrest hit factories in the Malaysian state of Negri Sembilan. Workers in several factories claimed they had been constructed on sites inhabited by demons. In a shoe factory on such a site, a woman worker suddenly started screaming, tore off her clothes and ran around wildly. Other workers followed suit and within minutes the factory was filled with screams and work ground to a halt. It took three days and the efforts of a spirit healer, who sacrificed a goat, to get production rolling again. At least seven other factories experienced similar outbreaks around the same time.

CHARLES FORT records a pig-tail cutting panic in China in 1876. Beginning in Nanjing, the rumour spread that invisible entities were instantaneously cutting off people's pig-tails, generally instantaneously and without the owner's knowledge. The panic spread to Shanghai and Hangzhous, leading men to walk round nervously holding their pig-tails in front of them. Doctors offered charms and soldiers were stationed on the street. The use of acid to remove the hair was mooted as it was considered impossible for shears to be used without the victim noticing. Suspect included charm sellers (hoping to boost business), mischievous children, missionaries etc, but no one was ever caught.

CHAPTER FIFTEEN

Completely Barking!

Insanity is no laughing matter, but….

A PET GOAT was apparently behind the attack which Negusa Negaste carried out on Open University official Peter Yates. Negaste laid into Mr Yates with a five-foot high wooden cross after demanding accommodation from the University, giving him a wound which required three stitches. When tried at Cambridge Crown Court, Mr Negaste explained that he was acting on the instructions of his goat, who was present at the incident and had alleged that Yates was a "murdering cannibal". He was ordered to receive treatment from a mental institution.

THE POLL TAX presented one Yorkshire resident with an insurmountable problem. A sufferer from multiple personality disorder, he had great difficulty in completing the form as he felt his disability meant that he was actually sharing his house with 17 other people, including an 18th century Albanian Crown Prince. His problem was that he could not be sure which, if any, of these individuals was liable to pay tax.

HE MAY have avoided a trip to the courts, but this was furthest from the mind of Brenda Butler Bryant. She filed over 700 lawsuits in one year and was ordered to stop until she hired a lawyer or found a doctor to certify that she is mentally competent. The Philadelphia woman had sued Burger King, the CIA, the University of Pennsylvania and the Philadelphia school board, among others. The main reason for forcing her to stop was that her lawsuits were, according to Judge John Fullam, “incomprehensible rubbish”. He pointed out that none of her hand-written lawsuits contained any complete sentences - one read “Slavemaster Service B/S Wholesale Club, Lane Bryant, Negro Services, BBB/KKK/LLL-Linda Lovelace/AAA”. In every case Mrs Bryant asked for a waiver of the $120 filing fee, often claiming to have been injured in a car accident the previous Mother’s Day. Her response to the judge’s ruling ? - she filed a lawsuit against him.

THE HONG KONG government’s biggest land sale was thrown into confusion when a penniless woman made a winning bid of almost £70 million for a plot. She was identified as someone who stood outside Legislative Council meetings shrieking at members, and was taken away in an ambulance.

MEMBERS OF Depressives Anonymous got even more depressed after cheerful people started turning up at the weekly meetings of their Gloucestershire branch. Chairman of the group John Hooper said “We did not foresee that the group itself would develop its own severe personality problem". Happy people were asked to stay away "Those with sensitive tender feelings have been put off by more robust members who have not always been true depressives." Hooper explained.

AN UNNAMED bus driver was transporting 20 mental patients from Harare to a mental hospital in Bulawayo, Zimbabwe, when he stopped for a few drinks at an illegal road-side bar. Returning to the bus he found that the mental patients had escaped; so he went to the nearest bus stop and offered free rides to 20 people. These he delivered to the hospital and informed the staff there that they were easily excitable. It took medical personnel three days to uncover the foul play. The real patients were still at large, according to this dubious yarn.

DANISH TAXI DRIVER Jorgen Gilberg accepted a booking from an elderly Dane for a 2,600 mile round trip from Copenhagen to the Vatican. When they arrived, the man explained that he had to collect the £2,500 fare from the Pope, who owed him £4,400. Then he admitted that the voices in his head might have misled him. "I had to laugh" said Gilberg. "I couldn't get angry with a man who was not playing with a full deck." So he drove him back to Copenhagen.

TV WEATHERGIRL Ulrika Jonssen was bombarded by obscene calls and nude photos of himself by Peter Casey who thought her weather reports were coded messages of love.

TEACHERS at Henry Cort Community School in Fareham, Hampshire were on the alert after children reported a strange intruder in the school grounds. A man described as between 30 and 40 with short grey hair and wearing a blue shirt, blue and white jacket and green gloves, leapt over the fence into the pond area and began drinking from the pool. He then cavorted in front of the children flapping like a duck and jumping like a kangaroo - when challenged by the Deputy Head the man scurried away at speed on all fours.

IN PECKHAM, South London, Anthony Smyth, 33, was seen eating daffodils, barking and chasing ducks with his pet terrier in London's St. James's Park, before barking at a party of Streatham schoolchildren, grabbing the bottom of one parent and lunging at a teacher's thigh. He was arrested and bit three policemen at Rochester Row police station. One needed an anti-tetanus jab for a serious bite after Smyth tore through his trousers. Answering a distress call in Roanoke, Virginia, police found a naked man wearing a dog collar, standing on the roof of a shed howling and shouting. Trying to put the cuffs on the man, officer E.L.Mills was bitten on the hand. Neighbours said the man and a group of dogs had been chasing cars and digging up gardens. "It wasn't just the man who thought he was a dog, "said Mills "the dogs seemed to think he was a dog too. It was uncanny."

IT'S A GOOD JOB neither of these guys ever came across Amela Lafeye, 67, of Dijon, France. Neighbours reported her to authorities after she was seen on her window ledge growling and hissing at a cat , which was growling and hissing back. Police found her on all fours. "She backed up and began hissing at us when she saw us" said an officer. "She has obviously gone mad from years of being deprived and alone and living on a diet meant for animals," said psychiatrist Dr Maurice Claren. "She apparently started eating (cat food) when her cat died and since she was very poor, it eventually became her regular diet. Of course it was not the cat food which made her behave this way. She has severe psychiatric problems."

ROAD RAGE is not confined to those in cars. A stressed-out Thai traffic cop, charged with controlling traffic at one of Bangkok's worst crossroads nicknamed "Hell Intersection" by local motorists, freaked out and turned all the traffic lights green. He was found dancing frenziedly amidst the ensuing chaos and was taken to a psychiatric institution where severe stress-induced mental illness was diagnosed. In Sydney, Australia, a man was found standing in busy traffic on a multi-lane highway, trying to touch his toes. When a policeman approached him the man lashed out, landing a shattering kick in the cop's groin, rendering him unfit for duty. No one had any idea why the man, provisionally identified as Robert Rynan, was there, as after being arrested he refused to utter a word.

THIS WOULD have suited psychiatrist Oscar Dominguez fine. Dominguez, 45, shot dead a woman patient in his Sao Paulo office as she told him about her sex life. "I just couldn't take those nutcases anymore", he told a court, where he faced a 25 year sentence.

THOMAS PASSMORE of Norfolk, Virginia, cut off his hand because he thought it was possessed by the devil, then refused to let surgeons at Sentara Norfolk General Hospital reattach it. He later sued them for $3 million, saying they should have known he was crazy. In Delaware, Bernadette French, 36, a manic depressive, sued Wilmington Hospital for $1.1 million and won after she gouged her own eyes out. She contended hospital staff had not supervised her properly. Taking similar action, but, as far as we are aware, not suing anyone was a 23-year-old unemployed man in Gosport, Hampshire, who cut off his tongue, gouged out an eye and stabbed himself in the groin in a fit of despair.

FOLLOWING COMPLAINTS of suspicious behaviour, Aaron Millar, 23, was arrested in Victoria, British Columbia. He was dressed in full army fatigues with a helmet and gas mask. He was also wrapped in tinfoil, to protect himself from alien radiation, he explained. He was carrying an imitation Molotov cocktails - antifreeze cans filled with water - and two knives. He had cut satellite cables at the Times-Colonist newspaper and CHEK Television, possibly in an attempt to halt communication with outer space. He didn't offer an explanation which made much sense, according to Victoria Police Staff Sgt Wayne Coleman."I am led to believe he felt there was alien movement. I'm not sure what that means," he said. Millar was sent for a psychiatric examination.

THREE FISHERMEN rescued Robert Slutsky, 54, from a cold sea 2 miles (3 km) off Long Island, New York. Raymond Keyes who fist spotted Slutsky bobbing along, asked if he needed help. The large man replied calmly "No, I'm just out swimming." He was wearing a flannel shirt over a T-shirt and boxer shorts. There were no other boats in sight. Doctors said that the natural bulk of his 300lb (136kg) weight had protected him from the cold water and kept him afloat for about an hour. "He was blue and floating in and out of consciousness," said Daniel Baudoin, one of his rescuers "We asked him his name and all he kept saying was 'Bob, Bob, Bob'. He might have been in shock." Slutsky had returned home from a Caribbean cruise the evening before he was fished out the sea. Early the next morning, he told his mother (with whom he lives) he had stomach ache and was going for a walk with their two dogs. The dogs came back on their own; Slutsky had no idea how he ended up in the water. His sister pointed out he suffered from diabetes and might have fallen victim to a diabetes-induced mania.

IN WHAT SEEMS to have been a bizarre attempt to evade a court appearance on a drink-drive charge, Dale Elder, 22, walked into a police station in Columbus, Ohio, on the day he was to be tried and announced "I need an x-ray. I want to make sure I have a brain." Then he reached up and began tugging at a wire protruding from his forehead "Blood started to trickle down it" said desk officer Dan Canada, "at first I thought he was pulling his hair. Then I realised it was a wire and I yelled 'Hey, Sergeant!'" Elder pulled out about three inches of the wire before the officers handcuffed him. They took him to Grant Hospital where he was stable after doctors removed the remainder of the wire. Elder said he had drilled the hole in his head and slid the wire inside to see if he had a brain. He felt no pain throughout the adventure.

PETER BOWEN, a disciple of American right-winger Lyndon LaRouche, and unsuccessful candidate for governor of Missouri, made an increasingly crazed speech to an audience of students at McKendree College, Lebanon, who grew angrier throughout. After attacking rock music for stimulating "sexual frenzy", sheep for spreading AIDS by coughing, Buckingham Palace for holding "homosexual parties upstairs" and the FBI for framing LaRouche followers in a credit card fraud scandal, he climaxed with the statement that the mark on Soviet leader Mikhail Gorbachev's forehead was the "Satanic mark of the Beast" mentioned in Revelations. His Proof? "Gorbachev insists that he always be photographed wearing a hat."

A MOTORIST stopped at a routine police check in Colchester, Essex, was found to be wearing wellington boots filled with baked beans in tomato sauce. "We have no idea why he was doing it," said a police spokesman, "but it is an offence not to be in proper control of a car. Wearing boots full of baked beans could cause the driver to be distracted and have an accident." The driver was released after a warning.

A GUNMAN who held up 21 people and forced them to whistle Hail, Hail, the Gang's All Here was being hunted in Alaska. He had never hurt anyone or stolen any property.

References

OVER THE EDGE

Mystery bombs *D.Star* 11 Nov 1994, *D.Mirror* 19 Mar 1990. Mini mystery *Sussex Eve. Argus* 18 Oct 1994. Lock loony *National Enquirer* 9 Jul 1991. Uninvited guests *Middlesborough Evening Gazette* 9 Aug 1997. Knobby tree *NY Post* 2 Jan 1992. Bridal tree *Liverpool Echo* 4 Apr 1995.Giant baby *NY Times* 21 Aug 1994. Animal abandonment *D.Mirror* 29 Feb 1996, Guardian 3 Sept 1994. Non-thefts *D.Star* 11 Sept 1991, *Dominion (Wellington, NZ)* 25 Aug 1992. *Batman People* 4 Nov 1990. Boggling burglaries *S.Mail* 10 Aug 1997, Sussex Express 7 Nov 1997. Weird walkies *[NZPA]* 11 May 1996. Mass painting *D.Telegraph* 28 Sept 1995. Left shoes *North County Register (Hamilton Ontario)* Jun 1996. Shoe dropping club *Sussex Eve. Argus* 21 Sept 1993. All at sea *Times* 11 Apr 1997. Wire sneakers *Dallas Morning News* 2 Mar 1997. Tree man *Pretoria News* 23 Oct 1979. Oh boy, one king *Jacksonville Journal* 13 Jul 1977. Lawn dumper *FHM* via *Guardian* 30 Oct 1997. Face licker *Courier-Mail* (Brisbane, Australia) 2 Feb 1998. Chopping spree *Newcastle Journal* 7 Apr 1998.

FAMILY FORTUNES

Eel beat again *D.Record* 11 Dec 1995, *D.Record* 14 Aug 1997. The silent treatment *People* 19 Oct 1997, *D.Express* 10 Sept 1992. Daft divorces *D.Record* 27 Oct 1995, *D.Star* 12 Apr 1994, *D.Star* 28 Jan 1994, *D.Record* 24 Jun 1994, *D.Star* 26 Jun 1991. Stubborn bastard *[AP]* 10 Feb 1994. Tit for tat *D.Star* 9 Dec 1993. Savage splits *Sun* 18 Mar 1994. Diabetic dog *Weekend Telegraph* 7 Jun 1997. Veiled horror *D.Telegraph* 3 Nov 1997. Nuclear widow *The Weekly News* 15 Jan 1994. Horse hitch *D.Record* 28 Sept 1992, *[AP]* 21 Aug 1989. Dead lucky *Edinburgh Eve. News* 24 Feb 1992, *Eve Standard* 21 Nov 1991.Stored stiff *D.Star* 17 Feb 1998, *D.Mirror* 14 Oct 1992. Dig 'em up *[R]* 26 Dec 1996, *Guardian* 5 Oct 1996. Yo-yo stiff *[R]* 14 Sept 1992. Family firm *Toronto Globe &Mail* 2 Apr 1992.

PROUD TO BE DIFFERENT

Swordsman *Eve. Standard* 28 Sept 1995. Draughty hobby *D.Star* 28 Feb 1995, *S.Mail* 14 Jan 1996. Aussie Ark *S.Mail (Scotland)* 27 Sept 1992, *Journal (Lincoln, Nebraska)* 17 Apr 1992. Vote Antichrist *Richmond & Twickenham Times* 19 Jan 1996. Wear hats! *Guardian* 27 Nov 1993. Giant baby *News of the World* 11 Nov 1990. Beany *D.Mirror* 13 Aug 1992. Loafer *Times* 13 Jun 1996. Tree bloke *Weekend Telegraph* 3 Aug 1996. Other tree bloke *Brisbane (Australia) Courier Mail* 27 Feb & 11 Mar 1992. Starer *D.Express* 20 Feb 1986. In print *The Oregonian* 28 Aug 1997. Unknown, *Sun* 19 Feb 1986 *Weekly World News* 11 Feb 1986 *FT 75:50*. Not a coffin dodger *D.Telegraph* 3 Jul 1997.

DUMB OR DUMBER

Alien sex fiend *The Sun* 7 Jan 1994. Loopy laws *D.Mail* 22 Sept 1997. Dogs dinners *Independent on Sunday* 8 Jan 1995. Lion lashed *Sun* 26 Mar 1994. Pant scoffer *Western Morning News* 15 Mar 1994. God not in control *D.Mirror* undated. Going nowhere *D.Telegraph* 27 Nov 1990. Stuck to it *D.Star* 4 May 1994, *NY D.News* 28 Feb 1993. Stuck dicks *D.Mirror* 7 Feb 1996, *D.Mirror* 21 May 1996. Free willy *Sun* 29 Jul 1997, *[AFP]* 10 Feb 199, *Sun* 23 Jan 1998.DIY medicine *S.Mail* 30 Oct 1994, *Sun* 26 May 1994, *D.Record* 14 Sept 1992. Dumb patients *S.Mail* 7 Feb 1993, *Doctor* 16 Nov 1995. Fly guy *[R]* 11 Jul 1991. Daft as a brush *D.Record* 30 Jan 1996. Eelectricity People 1 May 1994. Cash cockups *D.Record* 12 May 1994, *D.Star* 19 Feb 1994. Spoil sport *Weekend Telegraph* 27 Aug 1994. Floral failure *Times* 28 Mar 1980. Fascist physics *[AFP]* 5 Jun 1996. Al Nino *Independent* 3 Mar 1998.

CONSPICUOUS CONSUMPTION

Chote choke *People* 22 Jan 1995. Ear cure *Independent* 29 Aug 1998. Fart plague *S.Sport* 29 Sept 1991, Bangkok *Post* 1 Jul 1992. Human engine *D.Mirror* 31 Aug 1989. Gas huffer *Kayhan* 12 Nov 1997. Industrial drink *Source unknown*. Etheromania Letter *FT66:65* Dec

1992/Jan 1993. Cryogenic cock-up *British Interactive Group Newsletter* Spring 1998. Drinkers *Nottingham Eve.Post* 5 Aug 1992, *D.Mirror* 14 Aug 1989. Soft drink addicts *Sun* 5 Dec 1989, *Victoria (BC) Times-Colonist* 19 Apr 1995. Sponges *Sun* 18 Aug 1988, *Sun* 22 Apr 1988. Brain scoffer *D.Record* 28 May 1997. Fag stuffer *S.Mail(Scotland)* 12 Jul 1992. Rubber lover *USA Today* 17 Aug 1993. Roses n'silk *S.Mail* 17 Sept, 8 Oct 1995. Alternative intoxicants *S.China Morning Post* 27 Jan 1992, *Philadelphia Inquirer* 12 Sept 1994.Chasing the lizard *S.China Morning Post* 14 Jan 1993. Drug swallowers *Edin Eve News* 8 Jan 1992, *People* 6 May 1994. Foetus eaters *D.Telegraph* 13 Apr 1995. Toast trouble *Victoria (B-C) Times-Colonist* 6 Oct 1997.

TAKE THAT!

Piranha puncture *S.Express* 26 Apr 1995. Glow job *D.Record* 16 Jan 1995. Dicksoff *D.Mirror* 28 Apr 1995, *Independent* 6 Jun 1996. Weird muggers *S.Mail* 8 Jun 1997, *S.Mail (Scotland)* 16 Mar 1997. Chicken trouble *Middlesborough Eve. Gazette* 3 May 1996. Bat smack *Cox News Service* 15 Jul 1994. Chicken shit *NZPA* Date unknown. Dog attacks *S.Mail* 5 May 1996, *NY Post* 1 Feb 1991. Roach raid *D.Star* 25 Aug 1994, *D.Record* 8 Jan 1992, *D.Telegraph* 13 Nov 1991. BO raid *Brisbane Courier-Mail* 19 Jun 1992. Tyres'n tanks *Great Barr Chronicle* 3 Nov 1995, *USA Today* 22 Nov 1994. Shaver *Tonight* 27 Oct 1994, *Hartford (CT) Advocate* 11 Nov 1993. Sax maniac *Expressen (Sweden)* 23 Mar 1997, *Knight-Ridder News Service* 4 Nov 1993, *[AP]* 2 Aug 1992. Criminal contaminations *S.China Morning Post* 15 Nov 1991, *Washington Post* 25 Jul 1994, *Middlesborough Eve. Gazette* 19 Jul 1990. Food flingers *The Economist* 1 Oct 1994, *People* 11 Sept 1994, *D.Mirror* 31 Aug 1990, *D.Telegraph* 6 Mar 1991, *D.Record* 6 Jul 1994. Red hot jabber *D.Telegraph* 21 Nov 1991. Doughnut hurlers *San Jose Mercury News* 11 May 1994. Koala killer *Washington Times* 12 Sept 1993. Siamese violence *D.Star* 21 Apr 1993. Self abuse *D.Mirror* 23 May 1994. Monk Rumble *[CP]* 10 Sept 1997. What's the frequency, Dan? *[AP]* 31 Jan 1997. Molesters *Western Morning News* 10 Jun 1996,

Meridian News 16 Mar 1997, *Coventry Eve. Telegraph* 17 Sept 1996. Doll ripper *D.Record* 15 Jan 1993, *D.Telegraph* 30 Sept 1989.

INSANE CLOWN POSSE

Dodgy clowns *Denver Post* 17 Mar 1996. Violent clowns *People* 3 Jan 1993. Violent face painters *Edinburgh Eve. News* 14 Jan 1992. Stone clown *Bury Free Press* 29 Mar 1996. Wifenapper *D.Record* 5 Feb 1996, *Ogden(UT) Standard-Examiner* 23 Jul 1996. Gun clown *D.Mirror* 28 May 1990, *Independent* 17 May 1991. Shoplifting clown *Edinburgh Eve. News* 9 Jun 1994, *Sun* 16 Dec 1976. Farmyard fracas *D.Mirror* 17 Mar 1990. Grim Peeper *D.Star* 17 Nov 1994. Satanic Santa *China Daily* 25 Dec 1992. Bandit clowns *Various sources* 1994, *Washington Times* 7,8,9 & 11 Jun 1994. Porn clown *D.Express* 11 Jun 1987. Pepsi clown *Prince George's Journal(MD)* 13 Jun 1994. Gorilla clowns *Coventry Eve. Telegraph* 24 Feb 1994. Echoes of the Bunnyman *Fate (UK)* Aug 1971. Pizza fracas *D.Star* 25 Aug 1991.

SMASH IT UP!

Wallpapered *Sussex Eve.Argus* 8 Oct 1994. Pig painters *S.Telegraph* 14 Sept 1997. Renate fan *D.Star* 30 May 1994. Toilet terror *S.Mail (Scotland)* 23 Jun 1991.Sofa slasher *Independent* 23 Oct 1997. Flower fiend *Southampton D.Echo* 2 Jun 1997 Wallbanger *Sun* 24 Aug 1977. Headbanger *NY Post* 16 Jul 1991. More headbangers *D.Star* 14 Jan 1992, *Sun* 1 Aug 1994. Fairy vandal *E.Leader (Clwyd & Chester)* 3 Jan 1992. Lawnmover *Today* 4 Jun 1991. Weedwanker *SF Chronicle* 2 Jun 1987. Bookrippers *Sun* 15 Aug 1992, *Guardian* 14 Sept 1994. Library prude *Guardian* 14 Sept 1994. Dung flinger *D.Record* 3 Sept 1992. California crap *D.Mail* 25 May 1997. Fiat of pique *Northern Echo* May 1997. Sierra smasher *Eve. Standard* 22 Jan 1997.

PULLING THE WOOL

Flea market *S.Express* 12 Nov 1995. heart attaxi *D.Mirror* 3 Jun 1991. Biker buffalo *Indian Express* 7 Feb 1996. Buried truck *Sun* 10 Dec

1991.Laugh's a gas *Coventry Eve. Telegraph* 21 Jul 1994. Phone scams *S.Mail* 19 Apr 1991, *D.Record* 19 Sept 1992. Shoe cutter *[AP]* 12 jun 1992. Taxing identities *Middlesborough Eve. Gazette* 24 Nov 1989. No fixed aboat *D.Record* 21 March 1996. Radio silence *Source Unknown* 22 May 1990. Machine squirters *Independent on Sunday* 9 Aug 1992. Rude Rupert *Independent* 21 Sept 1991. Money for nothing *News of the World* 12 May 1996. Stealth exhibitions *D.Telegraph* 3 Feb 1997, *FT99:16* June 1997. That's no lady! *Ogden (UT) Standard Examiner* 12 + 21 July 1995. That's no man! *D.Mirror* 24 Mar 1992. Pregnant bloke *[R]* 24-28 May 1992. Exam mystic *D.Mirror* 23 Sept 1991. Magic pencils *Guardian* 15 Feb 1991. Height machine *Guardian* 13 Feb 1989.

LOST WEEKENDS

Unrescued Buddhist *D.Telegraph* 24 Dec 1996. Concealed children *NY Post* 24 Jul 1997. Rosemary's baby *Most British national papers* 27-29 Nov 1991. Hole hermit *[AP]* 28 Feb 1993. Freeway phantom *UPI* 14 Nov 1977. Bijou grave *Guardian* 15 Jun 1979. Time warp recluse *Guardian* 7 Sept 1989. Garden hermit *Guardian* 3 Mar 1992. Sheep human *D.Mirror* 7 Dec 1987. Headache *Eve. Standard* 25 Mar 1996. Porter's wife *D.Express* 19 Jan 1981. Chained up *Pretoria News* 21 Jan 1981. *Newcastle Journal* 21 Oct 1996. Shed mistress *D.Telegraph* 6 Jul 1981, *[R]* 28 Feb 1996. Evil world *New Standard* 7 Nov 1980. Daft dodger Omid Javan 12 Oct 1997. Thaied up[R] 7 Jan 1998. Imprisoned sisters [AP] 27 Mar 1997.

OFF THE HANDLE

Ramming speed *Edinburgh Eve. News* 29 Mar 1996. Thwarted musician *D.Record* 30 Nov 1995. Snapped waitresses *People* 19 Jun 1994, *D.Record* 13 Apr 1994. Kill 'em all *International Herald Tribune* 16 Oct 1992, Sun 10 Apr 1992. *S.Mail* date unknown. Gun dance *D.Record* 5 Sept 1992. Teacher trouble *Eve. Standard* 6 Feb 1992, Sun 16 May 1992. Shot it! *D.Mail* 24 Sept 1992 *Guardian* 5 Mar 1994. Sex frenzy *The Herald (Zimbabwe)* 2 Aug 1995. Tackle trouble *D.Star* 17 Jul 1995.

Religious severings *D.Post* 5 Jan 1995, *S.Mail* 4 Dec 1994. Hand horror *D.Record* 16 Oct 1992. Chicago hoax *Guardian* 11 Nov 1995. Teeth puller *D.Telegraph* 28 Jun 1989. No Choke *The European* 18 Nov 1994. Dumped family *D.Telegraph* 28 Aug 1996. Wet shots *S.Mail (Scotland)* 2 Aug 1992, *San Francisco Chronicle* 21 Jul 1992. Milk is murder *[AP]* 17 Aug 1992. Kareoke killing *Big Issue* 8-14 Mar 1994. Offal smell *D.Telegraph* 11 Jan 1994. Idiot day *Sun* 7 Oct 1996. Madness of sevens *[AP]* 7 Nov 1992. Not Happy *D.Telegraph* 15 May 1998. Handy protest *Independent* 11 Mar 1998. Nose slicer [AP] 10 April 1998.

A MAN'S GOTTA DO WHAT A MANS GOTTA DO

Calling a spade a spade *People* 6 Mar 1994. Egg-sessive *S.Express* 19 Nov 1995, *Washington Post* 1 Nov 1994. Serial Kisser *San Jose Mercury news* 12 Feb 1991. Priest-puncher *Direct Action no. 79* May 1992, *D.Star* 7 Jun 1993. Penguin passion *Guardian* 25 Jan 1997. Cuddly compulsion *D.Star* 25 Feb 1993. Bag of Nerves *Sun* 7 Oct 1992. Bike maniacs *D.Mirror* 10 Jul 1991, *Source Unknown* 10 Mar 1997. Kinky burglars *D.Star* 1 Aug 1994, *S.Mail(Scotland)* 11 Sept 1994, *People* 3 Nov 1991.Shoe snatchers *Fort Meyers News (Florida)* 29 Feb 1980, *D.Star* 10 Mar 1979, *Sun* 31 Aug 1978. Phone frenzy *Independent* 10 Apr 1997. Gonna get you suckler *[AP]* 23 Apr 1996. fishy-man *FT 86:18* May 1996. Home zoo *People* 29 Jul 1990. Big Urner *[R]* 22 Mar 1991.

WHO TOLD YOU YOU WERE NAKED?

Pond Jesus *S. World-Herald* 4 Aug 1991. Naked cop *NY Post* 12 Feb 1991. Naked came the stranger *D.Record* 9 Aug 1994. Joggers delight *Guardian* 21 March 1996, *E.Standard* 16 Aug 1984 *Sun* 7 Jan 1994. Dick decorators *Source unidentifiable* 24 Dec 1993, *Europa Times* Jan 1994, *[AP]* 30 Dec 1994. Lone Ranger's Tonto *D.Mirror* 30 Nov 1990. Naked bunnyman *Sun* 13 Dec 1991. Painting nudes *D.Record* 20 Jun 1994, *D.Star* 8 Feb 1993. Naked car thieves *Victoria (BC)*

Times-Colonist, 22 May 1988, *Duluth, MN, News-Tribune* 1 Jan 1990. Floydada outing *[AP]* 20 Aug 1993. Devil-driven *Melbourne Herald-Sun* 14 Jan 1997. Crash flashers *D.Star* 17 Mar 1994. Naked dancing *Black Country Eve.Mail* 1 May 1996. Cemetery tango *D.Express* 1 Aug 1988. Naked bush man *Western D.Press* 31 Jan 1996. Off the rails *N.Y.D.News* 6 May 1996. Naked swordsman *[AP]* 24 Mar 1997. Fast food flashes *D.Record* 15 Dec 1992, *Focus News* 14 June 1994. Spring Fever *Bangkok Post* 23 Apr 1994 *Guardian* 5 Apr 1995. Sex scams *D.Record* 8 Jun 1994, *D.Star* 25 Jan 1994. Strip cons *People* 19 Feb 1995, *Sun* 25 Aug 1984. Exhausted streaker [AP] 1 April 1998. Vegetable man *Standard-Examiner* (Ogden, UT) 1 Mar 1998. Naked bag bloke *Toronto Globe &Mail* 16 June 1992. Quacked up *Independent* 25 Apr 1992.

EVERYONE'S DOING IT!

Rolling & tumbling *D.Telegraph* 3 Oct 1995. Tossers *NY Post* 9 Feb 1994. Car baptism *S.Express* 24 Dec 1995. Gum goers *NY Times* 10 Jul 1996. Gone-nads *[AP]* 22 Aug 1996, *Hong Kong S.Post* 28 Nov 1993. Organ riot *Times of Malta* 28 Mar 1994. Shergolds *D.Mirror* 2 Jan 1991. Pepsi riot *Guardian* 27 Jul 1993. Tyre baggers *Source unknown*. Singing, Dancing, Crying *Edinburgh, Eve. News* 31 Aug 1992. Factory hysteria *Canadian Economist* 20 Nov 1993. Pig tail panic *Wild Talents Ch6: Charles Fort*.

COMPLETELY BARKING!

Got his goat *London Student vol14 (9)* 9-22 Mar 1995. Taxing problem *D.Mirror* date unknown. Lawsuits you sir *Toronto Globe Mail* 17 Nov 1994. Awkward auction *Times* 15 Oct 1997. More depressed *People* 26 May 1991. Barmy bus *Financial Mail (S.Africa)* 4 Apr 1997. Taxi taxed *Guardian* 15 May 1997. Weather signals *Guardian* 6 Jan 1991. Pond drinker *S'hampton D. Echo* 19 Apr 1997. Dogman *Guardian* 23 Jan 1988, *Weekly World News* 5 Feb 1980. Catwoman *Celebrity* 15 Oct 1987. Intersection frenzy *Source unknown* 1993, *S.Mail* 17 Sept 1995. Snapped psychiatrist *D.Star* 27 Nov 1992. Satanic hand chopper *Eve. Standard* 14 May 1996, *USA Today* 28 Feb 1994, *S.Mirror* 1 Dec 1991. Space warrior *Victoria(BC) Times-Colonist* 7 Mar 1997. Just call me Bob *NY Daily News* 20+21+22+27 Nov 1996. Wired *Columbus (OH) Citizen-Journal.*. Barmy politico *St Louis (MO) Post-Dispatch*. Bean machine *Times* 30 June 1998. Whistler *S.Mail* 8 Feb 1998.

WHAT THE PAPERS SAY ABOUT FORTEAN TIMES

"Possibly the most entertaining publication on the planet."
Wired

"My favourite magazine in the world, material or otherwise."
Alan Moore

"One of Britain's most determinedly peculiar magazines."
Daily Telegraph

"Fortean Times is wonderful."
The Scotsman

"Immensely entertaining... A great, roaring sense of humour."
Contra Costa Times

"Stories unfold with elegant understatement, and the most pompously-educated people are happy to be seen sitting down for hours with the Fortean Times."
The Times

"Mr Rickard and his co-editor, Paul Sieveking, carry on Mr Fort's work, bringing wit and erudition to outlandish subject matter."
The New York Times